MW01228321

HOLY SPIRIT WILDFIRE

How to Receive

The Baptism of The Holy Spirit

CHRISTIAN HEDEGAARD

DEDICATION

For him who has ears to hear.
*He who has an ear, let him hear what the Spirit says
(Revelation 3:22)*

TABLE OF CONTENTS

	INTRODUCTION	i
1	DEMONSTRATION OF POWER	1
2	LIKE A WILDFIRE	18
3	ONE HUNDRED PERCENT	26
4	A SIGN FOR UNBELIEVERS	37
5	YOUR MIND IS A THIEF	47
6	BAPTISM OR FULLNESS?	60
7	WHO IS THE HOLY SPIRIT?	70
8	FOR ALL AGES	80
9	WHY SPEAK IN TONGUES?	90
10	STRIVE FOR THE GIFTS	103
11	INTERPRETATION OR NOT?	115
12	THE TELEPHONE POLE	125
13	THIRST COMES FIRST	137
	EPILOGUE	145
	ABOUT THE AUTOR	147

INTRODUCTION

Every year, my wife, Karen, and I go on road trips to minister through the U.S. I think everybody should do this at least one time in life. America is such a beautiful country. We have everything here; oceans, lakes and rivers, mountains and canyons, prairie and desert. Every state has its own features and almost every metropolis is known all over the world.

When we drive through the landscape in the Midwest and see miles and miles of telephone poles that are planted along the roadside, it reminds me of church.

God has put us in the landscape as such poles to transport power and communication to people's homes, but many of us are not connected to the Holy Spirit who is God's Source of Power. Instead of connecting, we are just standing there, tall and upright, going through the tests, trials and storms of life, standing firm, looking for the day where Jesus will come in the sky and take us home.

This book is dedicated to all the pressure-treated poles that have a hard time connecting with the Holy Spirit. I was one of those, waiting out there, but nothing happened. I could not figure out how to connect because I was wired the wrong way with wrong teaching.

My prayer is that this book will rewire and empower you, that the Holy Spirit will come upon you and baptize you with fire with the evidence of speaking in tongues. I pray this book will open up this supernatural source in your life, so that you can carry the message of His power to your local community and the world.

Chapter 1

DEMONSTRATION OF POWER

But you will receive power when the Holy Spirit comes on you; and you will be my witnesses in Jerusalem, and in all Judea and Samaria, and to the ends of the earth (Acts 1:8).

Throughout the years I've heard many definitions of being a believer, but I still stick with the simplest one: to be a Christian is to be a follower of Christ.

Jesus is not asking us to knock on doors to share the gospel or to hold long, theological sermons, so that people will be intellectually convinced about His existence. Both can be okay, but it's not what really makes the difference.

What brings people into the Kingdom of God is the power of the Holy Spirit, a demonstration of His power working through our personal testimony, when we come as His witnesses and tell about what we have seen, heard and experienced in our lives.

We have triumphed by the word of our testimony (Revelation 12:11). When you tell people how Jesus has saved, healed and delivered you, people will start to listen. They don't want all the convincing and enticing words, but they are longing for evidence of Spirit and power.

Jesus is longing to demonstrate His power to people. He wants to fill us with the power of His Holy Spirit in the same way as He did with the disciples on the day of Pentecost.

It is the Holy Spirit that makes the difference. Before the Holy Spirit came, the disciples were sitting intimidated behind barred doors. But, after the outpour of the Holy Spirit, the same intimidated disciples were transformed into tremendous preachers who made an impact in their world by the power of the Holy Spirit with supernatural signs, wonders and miracles.

The Holy Spirit gave them power to testify. Not just to ring doorbells or stand in the town square in December singing Christmas carols and handing out tracts, but to share the gospel to people, to tell people about their crucified and risen Lord and Master.

They were witnesses with their lives at stake. They were willing to live and die for the truth. No price was too high compared to the sacrifice that Jesus had already paid.

For to me, to live is Christ and to die is gain (Philippians 1:21).

The Closet Christian

I was born into a Christian family in a country where you don't generally talk about God. My father was a pastor in the Pentecostal church and I was bullied in school because of my parents' beliefs. Everything outside the Lutheran church, which was the state religion, was considered a cult.

When I was saved in the early 80s, faith was a rare thing and, even though I tried to share my new belief with my friends, the opposition made me silent very quickly. As I went to the altar to give my life to Jesus, my girlfriend ridiculed me and stayed behind. She became a prostitute and I became a preacher.

At this time in life I didn't have the courage to step up and go against the mainstream, even though I knew deep inside that it was the right thing to do. I suffered from fear of man and was a slave to other people's opinions. You can say I was a "Closet Christian" walking around with my tail between my legs, instead of lifting my head high. I did not realize that God had called me to be the head, not the tail. (Deuteronomy 28:13).

As time went by, I realized that I wasn't the only one who had this problem. A lot of my friends from church felt the same way, except for a few that stood out. Those guys were on fire!

I noticed the difference and I soon learned what made the difference between them and us. It was the power of the Holy Spirit.

The word *power* in Greek is *dunamis,* which is defined as an explosive force, like a stick of *dynamite* that can blow up mountains. The English word *dynamo* is a machine for converting mechanical energy into electrical energy which is a transformation of power!

As I began to study, my quest became more precise. I was searching for the power to become a witness for Jesus Christ.

Seeking the Gift
When the fire of the Holy Spirit fell on the disciples, about 2,000 years ago, they all started speaking the language of the Spirit. The gift of tongues was an outward sign that there had been a change inside, a manifestation of the power of God, which could be seen and heard.

I came from a Pentecostal background where you believe in spiritual things. I was used to hearing how people would pray in tongues, even though I couldn't do it myself.

As I read in the Bible about the power, I wanted to receive the gift of speaking in tongues myself. So, I began to search for the gift, attending different meetings where I went forward for prayer to receive the gift of speaking in tongues.

Everywhere, people were laying hands on me and praying. One preacher said, "Open your mouth," another one said, "Lift your hands," and a third one said, "Open your mouth, lift your hands, and breathe deeply."

As I went to all these meetings, I really prayed to receive the power of the Holy Spirit, but nothing was happening. Instead of being filled with the Spirit I got more and more empty. With all these negative experiences it became difficult for me to receive the gift of the Holy Spirit and the gift of speaking in tongues.

"Oh God, please fill me with your power, fill me, fill me, fill me...", I prayed.

No one took time to explain to me how to receive this supernatural gift of speaking in tongues. At last, I felt convinced that it wasn't the will of God to fill me with the Holy Spirit, maybe because there was something totally wrong with me?

The Smell of Failure
Condemnation grew every time I went to a meeting. I almost didn't dare to go to the altar. It smelled like failure. It was too embarrassing to stand there when nothing happened. It took nearly two years in my pursuit of the gift of tongues until I finally got it.

Every year, our denomination would meet at a national convention and a lot of people would come to be filled with the Holy Spirit. It was almost a tradition that people could only get baptized with the Holy Spirit at the convention one time a year. I went together with my friend hoping that this was my year. Every evening I went for prayer. My friend and I were hoping to experience something supernatural. I was there for all the meetings except one and, when I came back the next day, my friend had received the baptism of the Holy Spirit without me!

Seeing my friend speaking in tongues made me even more desperate and I knew that it was now or never. At the end of the final meeting I rushed forward. As I stood there, someone from the prayer team came to me and asked what I wanted them to pray for with me.

"Baptism of the Holy Spirit, please!" I said.

As he laid his hands on me and prayed, I felt absolutely nothing, besides the fear and the shame of leaving empty-handed again.

The Unforgivable Sin

During the prayer, I was afraid to sin against the Holy Spirit or to mock the Spirit of God, which would be the unforgivable sin. I had never received any teaching about this, but I was convinced that God would punish me. If the words that came out of my mouth weren't from the Holy Spirit, but from me, the Heavens would open and lightning would hit me so that the cleaning crew could pick me up after the meeting in a dustpan.

The man from the prayer team continually tried to get me to speak in tongues. He said, "Just open your mouth and say something…"

I didn't dare to. I saw how he was getting impatient with me, so I ended up faking some words, just to get rid of him:

"Korra, korra", I stuttered.

"Good job, you now have it", he said.

"Now you just continue with what you've got."

I didn't feel that I had gotten anything. Absolutely nothing had happened. However, there was something in me that kept saying, "korra, korra."

After the meeting, I went home on my little scooter. It was one hour's drive, and I was doing the "korra, korra" the best I could underneath my helmet. All of a sudden on the way down one of the hills, a whole new amazing language came to me. It was almost like flying; I was singing, shouting, saying a whole lot of unintelligible words. I was so excited that the language of the Spirit finally was mine.

Myself or God?
When I woke up the next morning, I immediately started doubting the experience. I was sure that this was something I had made up by myself. But I had a longing in my heart to try again.

I found it was still working, even though my brain was protesting against the words that came out of my mouth, thinking I made all this up myself.

The following Sunday, I stood in the back of the church fearing that the elders would throw me out of the church if they heard my "tongues." I was so concerned about my tongues but still I couldn't keep my mouth shut. People started praising God all around me. I was nervous, but I wouldn't stop. I just kept praying in this new wonderful language.

After some days, my brain finally gave up reasoning. Every word that came out of my mouth was bubbling in my heart. It was such a great feeling, I didn't want to stop.

I talked myself out of doubt, and soon I knew that I had received something that was invaluable for my Christian life. It wasn't just words, but power. All fear and condemnation were blown away by the Holy Spirit dynamite that was working through me.

Power to Witness
Receiving the gift of tongues, the Holy Spirit gave me boldness. I became another person. I was not silent anymore. Now I was free to talk about my faith everywhere.

Soon my friend in business school was saved. I found out that I no longer needed an excuse for myself. Confrontation and opposition was still there, but now I had the strength to resist.

When this happened, I started to preach the gospel like I do today. At that time my life wasn't very holy, but the joy of being saved was so big that I just had to share it with others. My faith I used to keep to myself was now something that I "had" to share with other people, no matter what the cost.

All of a sudden, I had an enormous epiphany. In Denmark, we have a saying that "everyone is happy in their faith" and now I realized that this was a lie from hell. Truth must be preached. There is only one faith, one name, one mediator and that is our Lord Jesus Christ.

The Purpose
The reason God sent us the Holy Spirit is to make us witnesses, so that the gospel of Jesus Christ can be preached. That is what it's all about.

When I realized this, I suddenly could understand why I went through this in my mind and it became very clear to me why there was such discussion about this subject - the filling of the Holy Spirit or the baptism of the Holy Spirit, or how we will explain the manifestation of the Holy Spirit in our lives.

The will of God is for all people to be saved (1 Timothy 2:4), and that's exactly why God's adversary, the devil, will do what he can to silence you and me as believers. If he can prevent us from receiving power to become witnesses, the gospel won't be preached.

Satan hates when the gospel is being preached, and he rejoices every time he can ruin the work of God by turning the fire of the Holy Spirit off, through false doctrine and fear of man. He celebrates every time he sees Christians holding back, being shy and intimidated, without making use of the power that God has made available to all who believe.

Chapter 2

LIKE A WILDFIRE

Heal the sick, raise the dead, cleanse those who have leprosy, a drive out demons. Freely you have received; freely give (Matthew 10:8).

When I married my wife, Karen, in 1988, we travelled the world, visiting the continents of North America, South America, Australia, and Asia. As we were traveling, most of the time backpacking and hitchhiking around, we asked God to use us, and God started leading us to all kinds of people who were in need of the Holy Spirit.

We didn't really know what to do except to pass on what God had given us. Freely we had received it, and freely we gave it. Yet, I still held on to the idea that the baptism of the Holy Spirit would only happen at our church camps back home, in summer festivals and other major conventions. God showed me something else now that we were traveling around. It was only us, His witnesses, and a whole lot of people who wanted to experience God in their lives.

Our first Holy Spirit experience was with a young woman in Peru whom we met in a small village far out in the desert. She was about 20 years old, still living with her parents and working in their family restaurant. She was raised as a Catholic and was very hungry for the things of God, so we asked if we could pray for her to receive the baptism of the Holy Spirit.

As we laid our hands on her, she was immediately filled with the power of God and started speaking in a new awesome language. It was not Spanish or English. It was the language of the Spirit coming out like rivers of living water from within. Her face was shining. Tears were streaming down her cheeks. The more she spoke the more she cried. She spoke louder and got more words. It was amazing for us to see how she completely, without holding back, was able to receive the gift of the Holy Spirit.

That day, her life was totally changed. When I met her two years later she was in full-time ministry serving the poor people in the village. She was so happy to see me again and she asked me if I could pray for her sister as well.

More Manifestations
After this episode, Karen and I began praying for more people to receive the Holy Spirit. We got more and more excited when we saw that this was really working.

Every single one we prayed for started speaking in tongues!

I remember this young guy, who was saved, baptized with the Holy Spirit and healed the same day. He had a broken elbow and suffered a permanent injury but, when the power of God came upon him, he was healed instantly, so he could play the guitar completely without pain. It was a great miracle, and we praised God.

God's power spread. It was like a wildfire everywhere we went. We asked God to lead us to people who needed to hear about Him and we promised Him to pray for all the sick people that He would send our way.

One day in Lima, Peru, we met a woman in the street who suffered from polio. She was dragged along between her two daughters and asked if we could help her find a doctor. As we told her that Jesus was our doctor, they followed us back to our hotel. At the reception, we met two tourists and invited them to join us as we were praying for the woman. Both she and her daughters wanted to receive Jesus, not only as their healer but as their Lord and Savior. As we were praying, the woman and her daughters were saved and baptized with the Holy Spirit and praised God in new tongues.

After this, we gathered in a prayer of healing and commanded the woman to walk in the name of Jesus Christ. We had to hold her hands in the beginning but, after five-to-ten minutes, she was walking around without any support, while she was praising God in tongues. The two tourists were shocked. They were non-believers, but they had to accept the miracle that happened in front of their eyes when the woman was healed.

Street Meeting in Paraguay
We traveled to Bolivia and continued to Chile, crossed over to Argentina and ended up in Paraguay where we stayed for a while. Our plans were to buy a motorcycle and get on the road again but that did not happen as quickly as we planned. We lost control in the sense that the Holy Spirit took over, and the most wonderful things unfolded during the month we were staying in the capital of Asuncion.

We arrived in Asuncion just after the military regime's fall in 1988 and saw the coming of spring in a spiritual sense. People who used to live under severe restrictions could now gather freely at any time of the day, which they did. They moved their patio furniture out on the sidewalks, where they sat and drank tea till late at night with their neighbors. There was a nice, relaxed atmosphere, and we enjoyed being among these wonderful people.

As I bought my motorcycle, I went out to explore the capital on two wheels. One night as I was driving in the neighborhood, a dog ran after me and snapped at my leg. I speeded up, turned the motorcycle further down the street and stopped to pick up some stones to throw at the vicious dog. A group of people were sitting on the sidewalk with their tea cups staring at me.

"What are you doing?" they asked.

I started telling my story, sharing my testimony and preaching Jesus to them. It was almost midnight but everybody wanted to receive Jesus as their Savior so I went to get Karen to help me to pray. She was already in bed but I woke her up and, as we went back to that street, we led ten adults to Jesus.

Over the following days, they brought the sick to us from that street and they were all healed. A woman who had a paralyzed arm for eighteen years could suddenly use it again. She went home to wash her clothes and introduced us to her sister, who had pains in her foot, after a fracture where the bones had grown together wrong. She was also healed. The man in the house was set free from his alcohol abuse and the neighbor who had been suffering from sleep problems for years could now sleep like a child.

I did not know much of the Bible, only a couple of Scriptures, but my pious wife who came from the Lutheran church was teaching them and I helped her as I translated her preaching into Spanish. After a couple of weeks, most of the people in the street were saved and we were holding public meetings in a garage which became our first unofficial church plant, years before we started in full-time ministry.

Who Pushed?

What we experienced was the beginning of a revival. Karen and I talked about our little "church in the garage" and agreed that the next thing they needed was to be filled with the Holy Spirit. We were still struggling with our own religious ways of thinking, but we knew that this particular experience was necessary if all of these wonderful people were going to keep their faith strong.

I was wondering if it was possible to pass on the power that had changed me from being a Christian by name to being a follower of Christ. We decided to go ahead with the project "Holy Spirit baptism of the street's residents," which was going to be a very exciting experience.

Karen and I called for a meeting in our "garage church." We were very excited to see what would happen. She preached and I translated. Then we invited people to come forward for prayer. The first one we put our hands on was the woman of the house. She started to sway back and forth, talking with God in a new incomprehensible language. Then she fell to the ground and hit the floor under the power of God.

I didn't touch her and I actually thought that it was Karen who pushed.
"Stop doing that," I whispered.
She told me that she hadn't touched her either. I was wondering what was going on. I had never seen this before but I realized it was the Holy Spirit Himself who made the woman fall to the ground.

Later on, we prayed for her son who began to babble in a very unique language. He had been making fun of us previously, so it was kind of like God was taking him by surprise. He stared down at his mouth and was almost completely cross-eyed as he listened to the mysterious words that flowed out of his mouth.

That night, everyone was baptized with the Holy Spirit and, immediately, they all started speaking in tongues. As we saw this we received an increase of faith. We understood the Word of God was true and that our experiences could be documented in the Word. The filling of the Holy Spirit and the language of the Spirit wasn't just for the chosen, but for all: Catholics, South American Indians and backpackers. God has no favorites. He gives the Holy Spirit freely to all who ask.

The Scribes of Our Time
When we returned to Denmark after one year of travelling, we continued to do what we had learned on our honeymoon. We started praying for various people and found out that the Spirit of God worked in the same way here as abroad.

In spite of the strong Lutheran tradition in our home country, we witnessed how lives changed when we prayed for them to receive the Holy Spirit. Every time we prayed, everybody was filled with the Holy Spirit and received tongues as a sign.

By comparing our own personal experiences with God's Word, we came to the teaching you'll find in this book. Later I came to realize that there are people who read the Bible from a natural mindset and cannot understand what God's Word says about the Holy

Spirit. They don't believe that it is possible for all to speak in tongues. The conflict arises because they try to understand God with a natural mindset without knowing the actual dimensions of the life of the Holy Spirit. These people are the scribes of our time.

People can try to explain God's deeds, but no matter what they believe, I made a decision not to compromise. I can't and I won't take back the Holy Spirit and the gift of tongues from the people who received it just because some people think that it isn't biblically correct.

Chapter 3

ONE HUNDRED PERCENT

All of them were filled with the Holy Spirit and began to speak in other tongues as the Spirit enabled them (Acts 2:4).

I am so happy it was God himself who taught Karen and I on our journey around the world. I had heard theologians say that tongues weren't for all, but a gift of grace, which God gives to anyone according to His will (1 Corinthians 12:11). In those days, there were not many who dared to take themselves into consideration when it came to receiving the gifts of the Spirit. Many people think that God gives gifts according to their efforts and deeds.

We were taught that the gift of speaking in tongues was only for a particular group of people who were "chosen," and, in some ways, we believed that we didn't belong to that category. Because of spiritual inferiority we had reduced God to Santa Claus, who only shares gifts with the dutiful kids of merit and deeds, instead of reading what it really says. If God decided to give the Holy Spirit to anybody, why should that not include you and me?

When we studied Acts we read again, that *all* were filled with the Holy Spirit, and *all began* to praise God in new tongues. How many is *all*? You don't have to be a great mathematician to figure out that the Holy Spirit chose 100 percent. Why should it be different today? God has not changed. Jesus is the same, and the Holy Spirit is the One who works all in all (1 Corinthians 12:6).

The Pharisees in Jesus' time put God's Word aside to follow their own traditions. The same thing is happening today. The scribes and religious historians of our time have rejected the gift of the Holy Spirit because of what they have *not* seen. Some will even say that this gift has died out with the first apostles and, by doing this, they exalt themselves above the Word of God.

Tongues of Fire
In the beginning of Acts, we read about the coming of the Holy Spirit at Pentecost. The disciples were gathered to celebrate the feast in Jerusalem when the Holy Spirit manifested with a powerful blast of wind and tongues of fire in the house where they were sitting.

When the Holy Spirit fell, it was not just the twelve disciples who were affected, but *all* 120 of them, including Mary, the women and the brothers of Jesus (Acts 1:14-15). Tongues of fire sat upon *each of them*, without exception, which would be a total of 120 flames and Spirit-filled souls:

> *When the day of Pentecost came, they were **all together** in one place. Suddenly a sound like the blowing of a violent wind came from heaven and filled the whole house where **they** were sitting. **They saw** what seemed to be tongues of fire that separated and came to rest on **each of them. All of them** were filled with the Holy Spirit and began to speak in other tongues as the Spirit enabled **them** (Acts 2:1-4).*

It is understandable that the day of Pentecost is recorded in church history as "the church's birthday." The Holy Spirit made a powerful entrance into the world. People in Jerusalem were so touched by the situation that about 3,000 individuals were saved.

When the Holy Spirit came, it turned the life of the church upside down. At this time, there were Gentiles and Jews from all over the world gathered in Jerusalem. They were all wondering what was going on when the disciples began to speak to them about God's great deeds in their own languages.

Imagine being in Jerusalem at this time! This event was so loud and powerful, like the sound of a mighty rushing wind. It was so wild that the critics blamed the disciples for being drunk with wine, even though it was the early morning hour of 9 am. They did not know about the "new wine" the Holy Spirit was serving and, when Peter started preaching, he proved them all wrong.

Holy Spirit for Everybody

In Jerusalem, there were people who received the message. They did not doubt that the outpouring of the Spirit was the work of God. They were touched by the Word of God and wanted to be a part of the new thing that God was doing.

Peter explained that God had promised to pour out his Spirit upon every human being, no matter the gender, age or social status (Acts 2:17; Joel 3:1). And the people that were listening understood the Holy Spirit was not just for the disciples, but that the promise of the Holy Spirit also was for them:

*When the people heard this, they were cut to the heart and said to Peter and the other apostles, "Brothers, what shall we do?" Peter replied, "Repent and be baptized, **every one of you**, in the name of Jesus Christ for the forgiveness of your sins. And **you will receive** the gift of the Holy Spirit. The promise is for you and your children and **for all** who are far off—**for all** whom the Lord our God will call (Acts 2:37-39).*

Peter's sermon was for all - "Let *every one* of you be baptized" - so how can we read it differently? If the promise of the gift of the Holy Spirit was for *everyone* in the gathering, why should it not be for *every one* of us up to this day in distant countries and communities who, through the apostle's testimony, have experienced the same power - "for *all* whom the Lord our God will call."

I am convinced that *all* who were saved began speaking in tongues. It must have been the most natural thing to do, even though the gift of tongues isn't a premise to being saved!

God promised that *all* should receive the gift of the Holy Spirit. The outpouring of the Holy Spirit at Pentecost became the introduction to the Book of Acts, which I think should be called Acts of the Holy Spirit.

It was the Holy Spirit who worked through the apostles, so that the gospel was preached not only in words but also in power.

Phillip in Samaria

Ten years after the outpouring of the Spirit at Pentecost, we read in Acts Chapter 8 about Phillip's journey to Samaria where the Holy Spirit confirmed the Word with signs, wonders and miracles. The sick were healed. Demons were cast out and the whole neighborhood came to believe, including Simon the sorcerer, who was baptized.

The region of Samaria received the word of God, but they still needed to be filled with the Holy Spirit. It was like a double package. They had the Word, but they did not receive the powerful baptism of the Holy Spirit before Peter and John came and laid their hands on them.

*When the apostles in Jerusalem heard that Samaria had accepted the word of God, they sent Peter and John to Samaria. When they arrived, they prayed for **the new believers** there that **they** might receive the Holy Spirit, because the Holy Spirit had not yet come on any of them; they had simply been baptized in the name of the Lord Jesus. Then Peter and John placed their hands on them, and **they received** the Holy Spirit (Acts 8:14-17).*

Who received the Holy Spirit? The Bible does not give us names or numbers. The answer is "they." Those who received the hands, received the Holy Spirit. No exceptions were mentioned which would be all! It was so powerful that even Simon, the sorcerer, was amazed by the signs and mighty wonders he saw (Acts 8:18).

How do you think he could see the Holy Spirit? The Holy Spirit is only visible by the signs, which confirms He is there. I am convinced that it was the gift of tongues he saw. If you read church history, even the church fathers highly agreed that they were speaking in tongues in Samaria, and that the filling of the Holy Spirit and the gift of tongues were walking together side-by-side.

Peter with Cornelius

In Acts chapter 10, Peter went to go and see Cornelius and the people in his household. Cornelius was a holy man who was known for his prayers and alms. He had gathered *all* of his relatives and closest friends into his house (Acts 10:24) and, as Peter spoke the word of God to them, before he managed to lay hands on any of the those present, *all* in the house began to speak in tongues and praise God:

> *While Peter was still speaking these words, the Holy Spirit came **on all** who heard the message. The circumcised believers who had come with Peter were astonished that the gift of the Holy Spirit had been poured out even on Gentiles. For they heard **them** speaking in tongues and praising God. Then Peter said, "Surely no one can stand in the way of their being baptized with water. **They** have received the Holy Spirit just as we have (Acts 10:44-47).*

Let's look at the word *all* one more time. We know that *all* included Cornelius' relatives and closest friends. We don't know the exact number, but it was probably a whole lot by then. At least we can read that there were *many* people gathered in his house (Acts 10:27).

This was another culture and another time. I imagine a family gathering in Africa where everybody lives in the same village or nearby, with many more brothers and sisters than we will find in today's families in the western world. It must have been like this in Cornelius' house when the Holy Spirit came upon *all* (Acts 10:44), and *everyone* in the house began to speak in tongues and praise God.

The Bible does not mention that there were any exceptions. Speaking in tongues included *everyone* in the house. It was not an exclusive experience for the selected and chosen ones. Apparently, the people in Cornelius' house were *all* worthy to receive the gift from God. It was the gift of tongues that convinced Peter the Gentiles had received the Holy Spirit and, by this also, were a part of God's plan of salvation. First, they were filled with the Holy Spirit and spoke in tongues. After that, they were baptized with water.

The Church in Antioch
Another example of the evidence of speaking in tongues is found in Acts chapter 11.

> *Now those who had been scattered by the persecution that broke out when Stephen was killed traveled as far as Phoenicia, Cyprus and Antioch, spreading the word only among Jews. Some of them, however, men from Cyprus and Cyrene, went to Antioch and began to speak to Greeks also, telling them the good news about the Lord Jesus. The Lord's hand was with them, and a great number of people believed and turned to the Lord. News of this reached the church in Jerusalem, and they sent Barnabas to Antioch. When he arrived and saw what the grace of God had done, he was glad and encouraged them all to remain true to the Lord with all their hearts. He was a good man, full of the Holy Spirit and faith, and a great number of people were brought to the Lord (Acts 11:19-24).*

In verse 21 we read "that the Lord's hand was with them", some translations will say "The Power of the Lord was with them", which signifies there had been some kind of evidence, since a great number of people got saved! It was not by the convincing words of the

apostles but with a demonstration of the Spirit's power
(1 Corinthians 2:4).

In Acts 11:23 we learn that Barnabas saw what the
grace of God had done. How could he see something if
there was no physical evidence? Barnabas was a man
full of the Holy Spirit and when he saw the evidence of
God's blessing, he was filled with joy!

Paul in Ephesus

Twenty years after Pentecost in Acts chapter 19, Paul
traveled to Ephesus where he met a group of believers
who had not heard of the Holy Spirit:

> *While Apollos was at Corinth, Paul took the road
> through the interior and arrived at Ephesus. There
> he found some disciples and asked them, "Did you
> receive the Holy Spirit when you believed?" They
> answered, "No, we have not even heard that there is
> a Holy Spirit." So Paul asked, "Then what baptism
> did you receive?", "John's baptism," they replied.
> Paul said, "John's baptism was a baptism of
> repentance. He told the people to believe in the one
> coming after him, that is, in Jesus." On hearing
> this, they were baptized in the name of the Lord
> Jesus. When Paul placed his hands on them, the
> Holy Spirit came on them, and they spoke in
> tongues and prophesied. There were about twelve
> men in all (Acts 19:1-7).*

When Paul laid hands on the disciples in Ephesus,
they received the Holy Spirit as the most natural thing
in the world. They began to speak in tongues and

prophesy, not just a few of them, but *all* of them. The number is even specified. It says that "the men were about twelve *in all*."

Why would we think that it should be hard to receive the Holy Spirit today?

At that time, it was so easy to receive from God. The baptism of the Holy Spirit and the gift of tongues as a sign for the believers walked together. In other words, there was no baptism of the Holy Spirit without confirmation through the gift of tongues.

Paul received the Holy Spirit after God met him on the way to Damascus. First, he was hit with blindness, and God send Ananias to lay hands on him and restore his sight.

When this happened, he was *filled with the Holy Spirit* and recovered his sight. God did not only open his physical eyes, but his spiritual eyes were opened as well. We don't know if Paul was speaking in tongues on this occasion but we know that he had the gift (Acts 9:1-19; 1 Corinthians 14:18).

Conclusion
As we read about the first Christian church we see that the baptism of the Holy Spirit and the gift of tongues was for everybody. This is our Christian roots. As the church today, we should all pursue this kind of organic, authentic Christianity! On the day of Pentecost, the gift of tongues came directly from Heaven appearing as tongues of fire. Other times, it came by the laying on of

hands through the apostles and, in Cornelius' house, it fell on the listeners as Peter and John preached the word of God. We see how the wrapping of the gift could vary but the content of the gift was still the same.

Chapter 4

A SIGN FOR UNBELIEVERS

Tongues, then, are a sign, not for believers but for unbelievers; prophecy, however, is not for unbelievers but for believers (1 Corinthians 14:22).

Since we started our ministry, we have seen thousands of people being baptized with the Holy Spirit. Our first revival was in a Catholic Church where the children was filled with the Holy Spirit and started praying in tongues, even praying for their teachers at school!

I remember how two young guys were saved and baptized with the Holy Spirit during a worship concert as they were sitting in the pews. The power of God came upon one of them and he started to shake.

I asked him to come to the front. As he stood there shaking, his friend came and joined him. Both young men received Jesus Christ as their Savior and, immediately, they both started speaking in new tongues.

You have to understand that this happened in Denmark, a secular nation that had forsaken God, a country where kids in school are taught that God does not exist and where Christians who speaks in tongues are looked upon as mental patients. If it can happen there, it can happen anywhere!

One year later, we had another worship concert in the exact same place. Now these two young guys were sitting in the front row together with two other friends and, as we started worshipping together, I could see how they all were touched by the Spirit of God.

During the last song, we made an altar call and these young men's two friends stood up. It was obvious that they were not familiar with spiritual things, so I asked them to go with me to the back where they gave their lives to Jesus. After this, I prayed with them to get baptized in the Holy Spirit. Instantly, they began to speak in tongues, like they had been doing nothing but this their whole lives. These young boys had never been in church before but now they were filled with the power of the Holy Spirit, which made them fully equipped for their new life's journey with God.

A Desperate Man
After the concert, I told the worshippers and the band about these experiences. One of the musicians was looking very thoughtful. It turned out that he did not speak in tongues, though he had been in a charismatic church most of his life. He could not understand how these two young boys without any church background

were suddenly able to receive the gift for which he had been searching - for years.

Because of his own bad experiences, this musician had come to the conclusion it wasn't everybody who was supposed to be speaking in tongues, and he had even found some Scriptures that confirmed what he believed - or disbelieved! He was convinced that the gift of tongues was only for a few chosen, or only the special and holy ones. But now he understood that these two young people had received the Holy Spirit without any condition, except for repentance and faith in Jesus as their Lord and Savior.

That night he came to us, desperate, and, as we laid hands on him, he was filled with the Holy Spirit and began to speak in tongues. He called home to his wife and told her about his exciting news! Next time we met, my wife prayed with his wife and she received the gift as well.

The Spirit Shows the Way
Speaking in tongues is an outward manifestation of the invisible work God is doing on the inside. It is a sign for unbelievers (1 Corinthians 14:22).

The purpose of a sign is to show the way so you don't get lost. Every year, I travel thousands of miles on the road to preach the gospel and visit friends and churches along the way. The signs will tell me where I can fuel my car and where I can get food to eat. The signs on the road side show me what is available. When

I see the green and yellow sign with the word "Subway," I can almost taste my favorite tuna sub!

As Christians, we are called to be signs in a sick world so that people can look at our lives and see what is inside. People demand signs in order to follow. They want to see the power of God written all over our lives:

> *And these signs will accompany those who believe: In my name they will drive out demons; they will speak in new tongues; they will pick up snakes with their hands; and when they drink deadly poison, it will not hurt them at all; they will place their hands on sick people, and they will get well (Mark 16:17-18).*

Jesus didn't ask if we wanted to speak in tongues or not. He says that we shall do it! Not as a command, but as a natural thing as we follow the faith. It's the same thing with casting out demons and healing the sick. He does not ask us if we have the courage or the desire to do it, it is not an option. We just do it!

Some churches emphasize the *fruits* of the Spirit and forget about the *gifts* of the Spirit. We should have both. Just as the fruits of the Spirit should come naturally, the gifts of the Spirit should come naturally as well. Our lives must leave a trail of God's power and glory so that people outside the church doors can find the way into the Kingdom. Notice, the signs shall follow us. It is not us following the signs like people tend to do when they follow their favorite preacher around, all to experience the latest "Holy Spirit Zap."

Gift of Tongues

The gift of tongues is mentioned as one of the first supernatural manifestations, immediately after driving out demons. I don't think this is a coincidence. While the demons are being cast out the Holy Spirit can fill the space.

The devil will always try to prevent people from receiving God's good gifts - he will keep you in demonic bondage because he knows that when you first receive the gift of tongues you will grow instantly and start using the other gifts as well.

I have often seen how deliverance comes before speaking in tongues. One time, I was attending a seminar in a Pentecostal Bible College. We saw a couple of people who gathered to pray together over the weekend. I found out that one of the young men in the group was not baptized with the Holy Spirit. He felt like a failure and was contemplating leaving his studies at the Bible College just because he had not received the Holy Spirit baptism.

As we shared the word and laid our hands on him, he fell down on his knees.
"What is happening?" I asked.
"Dizzy," he mumbled.

I could hardly hear him when, suddenly, he threw up a big brown puddle as he was being delivered from an evil spirit. It was the spirit that had been hindering him from receiving the gift. Immediately after this happened, he began to praise God and speak in tongues.

The Big Fives

One time, I preached about "the signs" and used a pump gun for an illustrated sermon to bring the message through! I had five blank cartridges in the gun symbolizing "God's ammunition" which were the five signs from Mark 16:17. As I went through the Scripture, I shot the blanks off one after the other. This illustration made an impact. I don't think people forgot my message that day! In My Name they shall cast out demons. Bang! They shall speak in new tongues. Bang! They shall take up serpents. Bang!

Jesus is not talking about the religious snake handlers, like we find them in some areas of the USA. The snake in this passage is a symbol for Satan, "the ancient serpent" who was cursed and forced to crawl on its belly. When Jesus says that we shall step on snakes, it means that we shall exercise authority over Satan and the whole army of the enemy (Luke 10:19-20).

So what about the deadly poison, sign number four? This is not about jeopardizing our lives drinking poison. Instead, we should look into Scripture to understand the allegory. I found that the Greek work for drinking is *"pino"* which also can be used figuratively to mean: to receive into the soul. When Jesus stood at the temple and shouted to the crowds, that anyone who believes may come to Him and drink, nobody expected Him to give out water to everybody (John 7:37). He was using drink as a metaphor. Same thing with the poison. James 3:8 describes the tongue as a restless evil, full of deadly poison. Even if we "drink in" the deadly poison of the tongue, when we experience persecution and people are speaking bad about us because of our faith, it shall not hurt us. We are called to surpass gossip and scandal and not let these things affect our souls.

Healing of the sick is the fifth and last sign mentioned. Who does not want to lay hands on the sick, and see them healed? Jesus has called us to do so, even though you might not have seen it yet. That is why we need the Power of the Holy Spirit.

Notice these signs shall not only follow the apostles but all believers. Not just the pastor, the evangelist or the healing preacher on the Christian TV Channel either. We should all do the job of an evangelist (2 Timothy 4:5). God wants all believers to load their "gospel guns," to step out and exercise the faith that is found in the Word.

A Sign for Unbelievers

In Acts 2, the gift of tongues was a sign for people who did not believe. People of different origins were gathered in Jerusalem and each heard the Spirit speak in their own native language, like a personal greeting from God.

This is another side of the gift of tongues, when God takes your native tongue and make you speak in another native language instead of a heavenly language. What a mighty sign for an unbeliever to hear the Holy Spirit speak like this!

The first time this happened to me was in Israel where I was praying with a Messianic Jew. We were praying in tongues together and, suddenly, my tongue changed and it sounded like fluent Hebrew. The prayer turned out to be prophetic, spoken directly into her situation:

"You are like a beautiful flower in God's garden," I said and continued talking for a long time, speaking a very personal message from God to the girl.

I am not a poet so I would never have come up with this by myself. This happened twice in one week.

Some years ago during a revival, a woman came to the altar to receive the baptism of the Holy Spirit and the gift of tongues. It was difficult for her to receive, so I led her through the process, word-by-word, and made her repeat the words after me.

I could hear my tongue changing into another language. I had no clue what was going on, but the woman started to speak in tongues instantly. Afterwards, she told me that I had spoken fluently Italian. She had been living in Italy for 25 years and I gave her a direct message from Jesus in Italian!

I have heard people speaking Swedish without knowing it. I had been praising God in the Kenyan tribal language of Ljuja during a conference in London with African participants. One time, I spoke Tamil as I was praying for a Hindu woman bound by demons. She was slain to the ground, delivered and received the gift of tongues immediately. As she came running to me after the meeting she gave me the interpretation; I had told the demon in Tamil language to leave "In the name of Jesus Christ."

When God Shows up and Shows Off

People who don't know the language of the Spirit want to hear what it sounds like. I can understand that, and I will at all times demonstrate, because the Word says that tongues are a sign for those who do not believe. God uses the gift of tongues to convince those who do not believe in His existence, like He uses healing and deliverance to create respect. Signs make people believe and wonders make them wonder!

It is not our job to decide when it's the right time and when it's not, because God's thoughts are still higher than ours. He can take the greatest Gentile and heal him in front of a bunch of people, and then He can save him and baptize him with the Holy Spirit afterwards.

One time, I had a paralyzed man in my meeting who started walking. It was in a big congregation and I had a television crew following me. As I saw a group of Hindus with red dots on their foreheads, I knew the Holy Spirit wanted to do something special that night. I went over and started talking to the group and, as I found out the man was paralyzed, I asked the leader of the television crew to pray for him. The guy was not even saved, but I wanted to demonstrate how the Word is alive and how the name of Jesus is the most powerful name on the face of the earth. As I told him to lay hands on the sick and speak out His name, the man started to run.

When you experience these kinds of things, a fear of God comes upon people. It is like a rush in the pews. I love when God shows up and shows off. He proves Himself this way, especially when He baptizes people with no church background with the Holy Spirit in front of a group of religious church goers who would not believe in the gift of the Spirit, but change their belief system because of what they see. I don't think that God cares about how or where it happens. The only thing He is concerned about is that it actually happens. He is God, so He can do exactly what He wants to do.

Why do the nations say, "Where is their God?" Our God is in heaven; He does whatever pleases Him (Psalm 115:2-3).

Chapter 5

YOUR MIND IS A THIEF

*What we have received is not the spirit of the world,
but the Spirit who is from God, so that we may
understand what God has freely given us. This is what
we speak, not in words taught us by human wisdom
but in words taught by the Spirit, explaining spiritual
realities with Spirit-taught words (1 Corinthians
2:12-13).*

If you are one of those who have been praying to
receive the Holy Spirit and yet don't speak in tongues,
this book is for you. Persistence will wear out
resistance. As you understand the gift of tongues is for
everybody, you should keep searching for the baptism
of the Holy Spirit and the gift of tongues even more.
Don't give up.

I travel all over the world, and I've noticed that it is
hard for religious people to receive the baptism of the

Holy Spirit and the gift of speaking in tongues. Religion is man-made. You cannot comprehend the Spirit with your natural mind.

I have seen people with church backgrounds often have a harder time receiving the baptism of the Holy Spirit than people do who are outside the church. I realized that I had it the same way. It is all because of wrong teaching. In my case, it took two years to come to the understanding of what God had given me by His grace.

There was no angel flying down from heaven with a silver tuning fork and putting it on my lips to make them vibrate and speak out heavenly words. In my case, the man from the prayer team prayed, but nothing happened until I opened my mouth and started speaking out from my spirit- as I began to use the gift of the Holy Spirit, believing that God's promises also were for me.

The truth is, we can't receive the Holy Spirit with our intellect. We must accept that God *is* Spirit and we search for Him *in* Spirit and Truth the exact same way as when we were searching for salvation in Jesus Christ. Just like the message of the cross at Easter was received by faith, we shall also receive the message of the fire of Pentecost by faith.

When I opened my heart to Jesus, I did not see Him with my physical eyes and I did not touch Him with my physical hands. By faith I accepted the Word that was preached - and that's how I was saved. That is why no man can take salvation away from me. I know, that I know, that I met Him, even though science will say that I'm not saved, but rather hallucinating!

It's the same thing when you receive the Holy Spirit. You cannot see Him. You cannot touch Him. You have to receive the gift by faith.

Lunch Meeting in Kigali

Some of the greatest experiences I have had with the Holy Spirit have been on my trips to different countries in Africa where I have seen hundreds of people being slain to the ground at one time, even several times in one meeting.

One time in Rwanda, I preached in lunch prayer meetings in the capital city of Kigali. It was after the genocide in 1994, and the hunger for God's Word was great. I preached a whole week. More and more people came and, in the final lunch meeting, I think there were about 1,500 people in attendance. There were so many people present, there was no room under the canopy. People were sitting outside in the street, baking in the hot sun! And when the meeting was over, it was like a spiritual vacuum. People refused to leave even though the local pastors tried to make them go back to their work.

We realized it was the Spirit of God working in a supernatural way. Then we called forward to baptize people in the Holy Spirit, and soon 200 people were standing in front of the stage. It was wild. Demons were screaming and manifesting, and everybody was lying on the ground under the power of the Holy Spirit. Victims of the genocide were laying side by side with their executioners as they cried and prayed in new tongues. It was an amazing sight!

The Program Goes Haywire
On another trip to Rwanda I experienced something similar. I had been away from Karen and the children for several weeks. When we arrived at the last meeting on Sunday morning, I just wanted to go home.

I arrived in my best suit and was pretty tired when I was told that I wasn't going to be preaching in the church, but in a boarding school in the bush. I did not particularly want to, mostly because of the dust from the long trip in the car, but there was nothing to do about it. Soon I was on my way out to the school where I was going to preach to both students and teachers.

It smelled really bad where I was going to sit because the chickens were walking around in that area. The smell of sweat from 500 dancing Africans was in my nose and, when I finally went to the stage, the pastor told me that I only had 45 minutes to preach. I did not like that. I can deliver a short message but I want to have enough time to preach and minister to people if the Holy Spirit wanted me to do so.

What do you preach as an evangelist when you come to a new place? The Holy Spirit reminded me of Paul who said that he would look forward to coming and sharing a spiritual gift with the churches. I felt the exact same way. I decided to preach about the baptism of the Holy Spirit. Then I untucked my shirt and took off my tie so I could move about more freely!

I preached for exactly 45 minutes before I called for people to come forward for prayer. Instantly, about 250-300 people came to the altar, hungry for the baptism of the Spirit. The pastor looked at his watch, but, just before he was going to stop the meeting, the fire of the Holy Spirit fell upon the crowd.

People were knocked to the ground and fell upon each other as they were praying and shouting in tongues. I don't know how long they laid there, but I saw the pastor standing, desperate over losing complete control. People were laying everywhere and praising God. The ushers tried to remove people from the stage, without any success. The program went haywire. This is what happens when revival breaks out!

Switch off the Mind
Many Africans have a natural approach to the spiritual realm while we in the Western world have some intellectual difficulties. We want to study, analyze and dissect, forgetting that God's wisdom is different from people's wisdom. To receive from God is so easy. It is hard for the natural mind. If you feel that your brain is blocking you, switch it off and receive from God with the spirit man. It is by the spirit that we understand the divine dimension.

Where I was born, we have a bird that is known as a thief. The bird is a magpie. It is attracted to bling and will steal everything shining in the sun. If you lay silverware outside on the porch, the magpie will try to steal the spoons. If you put down your jewelry, it will try to steal the gold. It will snatch it up and take it to its nest where you will find it one day when you cut your tree down.

The human mind is like one of those magpies. It will always try to steal the spiritual "gold" in our lives. When God gives you His spiritual treasures, this annoying bird (the human mind) will show up and fly away with all the precious gold that was supposed to enrich our spiritual lives.

In our society, we celebrate the brain and value mental health. As we buy fitness memberships to exercise our bodies, so we must work out our soul, empowering our intellect by feeding it with all kinds of information through newspaper, television and social media.

Imagine if we made the same effort to train our spiritual muscles? Why do we like our spirit to look like a piece of weak, limp spaghetti? Praying in tongues will edify and build up your faith, as reading and hearing the Word will increase your faith muscles.

The Word of God teaches us that a "natural man," a person without the Spirit, does not understand that which comes from God, because it needs to be discerned spiritually:

> *The person without the Spirit does not accept the things that come from the Spirit of God but considers them foolishness, and cannot understand them because they are discerned only through the Spirit. The person with the Spirit makes judgments about all things, but such a person is not subject to*

merely human judgments, for, "Who has known the mind of the Lord so as to instruct Him?" But we have the mind of Christ (1 Corinthians 2:14-16).

It is impossible to interpret spiritual things out of human wisdom. Only by the Spirit do we understand the gift of tongues and the spiritual gifts which come from God.

Repeat After Me

When you seek the baptism of the Holy Spirit, you should expect that God will confirm the baptism through the gift of tongues, as in the time of the apostles. God will always give you the evidence of speaking in tongues and, if you do not begin to speak, it could be because of fear of man, unbelief or a mental block due to bad experiences from which you are unable to break away.

Understand that the devil does not want you to be empowered. He wants to keep you bound in fear and unbelief. He will tell you that it sounds weird and steal your confidence so that you do not dare to speak a language you do not understand.

When we went on our first road trip with our kids, it was embarrassing for them to speak with strangers in English. They practiced with us in the car. We spoke a phrase in English and they would repeat it. Eventually, they got used to the "strange" sounds and started feeling more confident pronouncing words in English. All four of them learned to say their names, their ages and where they came from, including our youngest son who had just turned five!

To speak the language of the Spirit is not the same as speaking in English or another foreign language, but some of the same mechanisms are still in play. When you speak a natural language, you speak the words that come into your mind. When you speak the language of the Spirit, you speak out of your spirit and express it through your mouth.

The key to a spiritual breakthrough is to overcome the obstacles of the soul. It is not about what or how you feel; it is all about what you believe. You have to open your mouth and start speaking. You have to bypass your brain.

Don't be afraid to speak out. Even if you think you are making it up, God will take over and give you words of the Holy Spirit as you open your mouth and speak in faith. Don't be afraid when people say "repeat after me" or even count to three. Don't let go before you receive.

When your mind tries to steal your blessing like the bird I told you about, the Holy Spirit is there to teach you. He will come when you call out for Him. He will remove the roadblocks of wrong teaching and lift you up to higher ground.

In 2 Corinthians 6:2, the Bible declares, "In the time of my favor I heard you, and in the day of salvation I helped you." Faith always works today. Today is the appointed and acceptable time. Do not procrastinate or push away what God has for you. The argument, "I cannot" does not work in this context, because "all things are possible for those who believe."

The worst thing you can do is to speculate, whether it sounds right, or even worse, to compare your personal tongues to the tongues of others. Tongues are personal! Don't try to figure it out yourself. You cannot understand the things of the Spirit with your carnal mind.

If God only gives you two syllables, then start with that. Even if it sounds like "da-da" baby talk! Don't worry about small beginnings. If He is satisfied with you saying two syllables, you should be too.

Walking on Water

I spoke with a young man in a meeting who had been prayed over for the baptism of the Holy Spirit several times during the last year without being able to speak in tongues. He was still waiting for "something" to happen and was irritated when people asked if he spoke in tongues or not. He thought that it could not be that important to speak "nonsense," especially when it was not being interpreted.

I started teaching him the Word of God and, finally, he saw what the Word said; that the gift of tongues was not just for the chosen ones. So, I laid my hands on his head and prayed a short prayer.

"Begin to speak in tongues," I said.

"I am gonna count to three"…

The young man understood that the ball was now on his side of the line, finding out that God already did it all. The rest was up to him. I asked him to stop speaking in his native language and challenged him to speak in tongues with me instead. At this point, he wanted to back out so he suggested that he go and pray at home. I urged him to stay. I did not want to let go of him and just leave him feeling like a failure.

Finally he decided to "walk on the water" by saying words he did not understand. Only a few words came out but what I heard was good enough.

"You just keep going," I said, and asked one of his friends from church to stand by his side and pray in tongues with him for another half hour.

It was obvious that he was still having a hard time. He was fighting the thoughts of false doctrine, but he still chose to silence the brain by repeating the words that he did not understand. He spoke and spoke. After half an hour, I came back to him to hear how it was going. He was whispering so I suggested that he turned up the volume.

He started talking louder and, in the end, he was shouting in tongues. That night was a turning point for this young man who had known Jesus since he was a child. Religious ways of thinking were being broken down and replaced with a new dimension of faith.

You know, God has given us different ways of expressing our language. We can whisper, talk, yell, scream, shout, and sing with our voice - so why not do the same thing when you express the language of the Holy Spirit?

Loud and Clear

I remember an evening where one of our co-workers was baptized with the Holy Spirit. Her husband got saved a couple of months before, and now it was her turn to take part in the new life.

When we started praying, it was like we hit a wall. Even though the woman wanted to be baptized with the Holy Spirit, she did not open up her mouth and speak. She only moved her mouth a little bit, and it was obvious that she was struggling. The woman was like a stone. My wife stood next to her and felt the woman squeezing her hand. She squeezed her hand so hard that my wife almost screamed, because it hurt. I did not notice but continued pressing on until the woman spoke in tongues fluently.

This woman went from being totally obstinate to loosening up more and more. Her pitch was still low, so we asked her to raise her voice to break through. Lastly, we stood together and sang in the Spirit. You could feel the spiritual pressure leaving and, even though we were tired, we did not want to leave. We did not go home until 2.30 am.

After we left, the man and his wife took another hour in the kitchen praying together and trying the new gift that God had given each one of them. Later she told me how she had been delivered through the baptism of the Holy Spirit. The resistance she felt came from past experiences of sexual abuse but, when she yielded to the Spirit, these strongholds in her life were broken and she was free to speak.

An Hour of Tongues
When you receive the baptism of the Holy Spirit, it is important to speak in tongues until you are familiar with it. I think everybody who has been baptized with the Holy Spirit should go home and speak in tongues loudly, an hour a day, for at least the first week until they get used to the new language. I personally speak in tongues all the time.

When you do that, you will find that time passes really fast. I have seen many people lock themselves in a room for several hours praying in tongues, just enjoying the presence of the Holy Spirit without being disturbed.

Paul said that he spoke more in tongues than everybody else (1 Corinthians 14:18). He also said he would rather speak five intelligible words to instruct others in the church than ten thousand words in a tongue. I guess he would not say so unless he had tried it. How long does it take to speak ten thousand words in tongues? I heard a pastor say that it took him 50 minutes. You don't have to count it, but one hour is a good span of time!

It is possible to speak in tongues, wherever you are. You can speak when you are alone with Jesus, in your room, in the car, or on a bike going to and from work.

You can also speak in tongues while driving, on a bus or train. It is actually possible to sit calmly and quietly by yourself and speak on the inside. No one will even notice that you are doing it.

My wife tells me that I speak in tongues when I am asleep. Sometimes I wake up in the middle of the night by speaking loudly in tongues and, when I wake up in the morning, the language of the Spirit is usually the first thing that comes out of my mouth. When I prepare myself before a meeting or a lecture, I speak in tongues all the time. I can even do it while reading the Bible. I can read the words and think about them while I pray in the Spirit. It is like I have two tracks. To speak in tongues should be as natural for a believer as is regular breathing.

Chapter 6

BAPTISM OR FULLNESS?

John answered them all, 'I baptize you with water. But one who is more powerful than I will come, the straps of whose sandals I am not worthy to untie. He will baptize you with the Holy Spirit and fire' (Luke 3:16).

Our understanding - or lack of understanding - of the Word of God can be a hindrance for the Spirit of God. My wife is originally from the Lutheran church. She was baptized with the Holy Spirit during the Charismatic revival in the 1970s. But she actually received the gift of tongues a long time before I did, in the Pentecostal church in the 1980s, which was contrary to everything I had learned!

I thought as a Pentecostal, thinking that "we had it" and that the Lutheran church "did not have it." But the truth was - she was much more free than I was. As I was living in sin and rebellion throughout my teenage years, she took part in starting charismatic prayer meetings together with her fellow students.

When she went to boarding school in her high school years, Karen told me there were many students who were baptized with the Holy Spirit. They began to speak in tongues without really knowing what it was that hit them. One of the girls began to speak in tongues all by herself while she was reading a book about the Holy Spirit!

What happened was the sovereign work of the Holy Spirit. Students repented from their sins and gave their lives to Jesus. Almost everybody showed up for Bible study to hear about the power of God. People prayed in classrooms and in their rooms until late at night and early in the morning at the library. When a lady from the staff came to clean around 7 am, she looked pretty disturbed. I guess she thought she was in the wrong place when she opened the door and found 20-30 young people gathered together in prayer!

It was like a wildfire that nobody could control. One night, the teacher of the German Language Art Department caught one of the young man in the hallway with a Bible in his hand after official bed time. The young man explained that he was going to a prayer meeting. The teacher obviously didn't believe it. The next day in class, she made fun of the young man. She did not know that this particular student had become born again. She thought his explanation about the prayer meeting at nighttime was a cover-up and called it "the lamest excuse," not knowing it was the actual truth!

Baptism of the Holy Spirit

The fire of the Holy Spirit is a revival fire and, when the Holy Spirit falls on people, revival breaks out no matter what denomination you belong to. God wants us to speak the language of the Spirit without reservation or preconceived notions.

Sadly, I found out that the expression "baptism of the Holy Spirit" meets resistance in many church circles because the only baptism talked about is water baptism done in the name of the Father, the Son and the Holy Spirit. I do not understand why the word 'baptism' is a problem when Jesus is introduced by John the Baptist as the one who baptizes with Holy Spirit and fire.

For John baptized with water, but in a few days you will be baptized with the Holy Spirit (Acts 1:5).

This Scripture is not about the traditional baptism with water, but about the baptism of the Holy Spirit at the day of Pentecost. The word *'baptize'* in Luke 3:16 is the Greek word *baptizo*, which refers to a complete immersion in another element.

The word *'baptizo'* is found in ancient Greek literature. The physicist Nicander made a description of how to preserve vegetables: To make pickles, the vegetable needs to be dipped (*bapto*) in boiling water, after which it becomes (*baptizo*) the finished pickle that we all enjoy eating.

What God wants to do in our lives is not just a dip but a radical work of the Spirit. When God is baptizing us with the Holy Spirit and we are getting transformed, our life with Jesus gets preserved and the vegetable (us) becomes a pickle (a new creation)!

Baptismal Doctrine

It is crucial that we don't let the word 'baptism' hinder us from receiving what God has for us. In some denominations, people learn that water baptism saves, and that everybody receives the Holy Spirit in water baptism. For this reason, people cannot receive the Holy Spirit again later in life. It is already done.

I find this to be very complicated, especially because the Lutheran church practices infant baptism which is not directly mentioned in the Bible, claiming this as the only truth, while the baptism of the Holy Spirit (which is mentioned many times throughout the New Testament) is something that they do not talk about.

What do you say to people that think they have it when you know that they can have so much more? You must use another language in order to reach these people, so we introduced them to "gift discovery" and would teach them how to unwrap the gift of the Holy Spirit as if it was a Christmas gift waiting to be received.

Just as with water baptism, Holy Spirit baptism has become a cause for dissension in many churches which is really sad. God wants us to have both; first, the baptism in water for the remission of sins and, then, the baptism of the Holy Spirit--receiving the gift with the evidence of speaking in tongues.

Peter replied, 'Repent and be baptized, every one of you, in the name of Jesus Christ for the forgiveness of your sins. And you will receive the gift of the Holy Spirit (Acts 2:38).

In Acts 8:14-17, we read how the believers in Samaria received the Holy Spirit after being baptized in the Name of Jesus Christ. Nobody told them to wait until they were mature enough or they had reached a certain age. This happened immediately after the water baptism. It was the practice of the early church and was done with the laying of hands on that person.

Baptism in Greenland
The doctrine of infant baptism is very dominant in certain denominations and, over the years, I have seen how it keeps people passive because they think that they got it all in the baptism even though they do not believe or live the Word of God.

Many years ago, we had a revival in the northwest part of Greenland. I went there on a mission trip together with an old Danish missionary and two Inuit translators. We spent almost 20.000 dollars to get there, traveling by airplane and helicopter to one of the most remote places on the ice called Kullorsuaq which means "The Devils Thumb." We were invited by a school teacher who had read my first book "Conquering Demons" on the Internet and translated it into his native language. He arranged our meetings at the local school and, as we arrived there, we saw the place was packed. People got saved, healed and delivered. It was awesome to see the work of God in that community.

During the revival in Kullorsuaq, Greenland, new believers repented and received the Holy Spirit, speaking in tongues. They were all baptized as *infants* but, as they started reading the Bible, they wanted to be baptized as *believers*. They arranged the baptism in a fish tub at the harbor and suffered great persecution from the Lutheran church for doing so. I did not baptize anybody in water but I made sure that they all got filled with the Holy Spirit before I left that place. They needed to be empowered and, after they received the Holy Spirit, they started witnessing and went by boat to preach to other remote villages, starting new churches along the coast.

The Inuits in Kullorsuaq still write to me and send me pictures when new believers get baptized in water and become filled with the Holy Spirit. Let us not go into a discussion about whether people need to be sprinkled or immersed in water. I would rather talk about the "rivers of living water" that flow on the *inside* of those who believe.

Born by the Spirit
The Holy Spirit lives on the inside of every believer who has received Jesus Christ as their Lord and Savior, even if they have not experienced an outpouring of the Holy Spirit with the evidence of speaking in tongues.

No one can come to believe without the conviction of the Holy Spirit.

No one can say, "Jesus is Lord," except by the Holy Spirit (1 Corinthians 12:3).

When he comes, he will prove the world to be in the wrong about sin and righteousness and judgment (John 16:8).

Remember the scribe, Nicodemus, who came to Jesus at night. He knew that Jesus was a great teacher but had no recognition of Jesus as his Savior because it had not yet been revealed to him by the Holy Spirit. He needed to be saved!

Jesus answered, 'Very truly I tell you, no one can enter the kingdom of God unless they are born of water and the Spirit. Flesh gives birth to flesh, but the Spirit gives birth to spirit. You should not be surprised at my saying, 'You must be born again' (John 3:5-7).

The new birth is the Holy Spirit's sovereign work. No one can see the Kingdom of God without being born again. The new birth is a divine intervention where God breathes His Spirit into our spirit and gives us life, new life. To be born again is the beginning of everything in the Kingdom of God, including the baptism of the Holy Spirit. If you are not born again, it can happen right now. Ask Jesus to come into your heart and cleanse you from all sin. He died on the cross for you. He took the punishment for your sins so that you could have peace with God. Jesus Christ paid the price with His blood. He made the way into God's heart, so that we, as God's children, can live in eternal fellowship with Him.

From Birth to Baptism
Jesus was born by the Spirit. The Holy Spirit was in Him. Then the Holy Spirit came upon him in the figure of a dove at his baptism, which was the start on his public ministry with healings and miracles.

Then Jesus came from Galilee to the Jordan to be baptized by John. But John tried to deter him, saying, "I need to be baptized by you, and do you come to me?" Jesus replied, "Let it be so now; it is proper for us to do this to fulfill all righteousness." Then John consented. As soon as Jesus was baptized, he went up out of the water. At that moment heaven was opened, and he saw the Spirit of God descending like a dove and alighting on him. And a voice from heaven said, "This is my Son, whom I love; with Him I am well pleased (Matthew 3:13-17).

How could the Holy Spirit both be in Him and upon Him? First of all, the Holy Spirit is omnipresent and He, the Spirit, works on different levels - first the indwelling Spirit by the new birth and, secondly, the outpoured Spirit, through the baptism of the Holy Spirit.

The disciples had their first experience on Easter morning after the resurrection. They received the life of the Spirit when Jesus showed Himself to them.

And with that He breathed on them and said, "Receive the Holy Spirit" (John 20:22).

We see how they already had the Holy Spirit inside of them before the Holy Spirit came upon them a second time with power in Acts 2.

If both Jesus and the disciples could experience this, why wouldn't it be possible for us today? Many Christians only know the first dimension. They have been born again by the indwelling of the Spirit which gives them part in the life of the Spirit and the Spirit's fruits. But they have not experienced the second dimension yet: The baptism of the Holy Spirit with the power of the Spirit, which equips for ministry and releases spiritual gifts into their lives.

Born, Baptized or Filled?

Let me finish this chapter by looking at the expression, "Filled with the Holy Spirit," (Ephesians 5:18). The word filled is a Greek word and is called *pletho*, and can be translated into the word complete or fully furnished.

It is not hard to recognize a complete building or a fully furnished apartment in the physical world. You would not move into a house with no roof, or furnish an apartment without having to buy the furniture first!

Still, there are Bible scholars who maintain the belief that being filled with the Holy Spirit comes with the baptism, even though no visible signs follow. Unfortunately, there are many sincere Christians who have been deceived into believing this. They say you have it. But it is like "The Emperor's New Clothes." It's a fairy tale with no signs in reality.

When Peter and Paul were filled with the Holy Spirit in the book of Acts, it was pretty obvious to everyone that many things were happening: *Filled by the Holy Spirit*, Peter held his defense speech to the leaders of the people and the elders of Jerusalem, and they finally had to let him go (Acts 4:8) and, *filled with the Holy Spirit*, Paul looked straight at the wizard Elymas (Acts 13:9) and prophesied to him so Elymas went blind and had to grope around.

To live as a Christian without the power of the Holy Spirit is to drive a car without gas. Until you add gas to the engine, there will not be a power transfer. There will be no spark. The car looks nice in the garage. It is fully equipped, but it does not get anywhere and won't bring any joy to anyone but the owner himself. If you want to take the car out for a drive, you need to add some gas! We need the Holy Spirit when the gospel is being preached. At Pentecost, the Word was being preached with power and accompanying signs. Something was missing before Pentecost, and nothing was the same after that day. The Holy Spirit made the difference. From here came the spark that started the apostolic era and birthed the Church.

Chapter 7

WHO IS THE HOLY SPIRIT?

But very truly I tell you, it is for your good that I am going away. Unless I go away, the Advocate will not come to you; but if I go, I will send him to you (John 16.17).

When we seek the baptism of the Holy Spirit in our lives, the Word of God is to show us the way. First and foremost, we must get to know the Holy Spirit, just the way we came to know God and Jesus. The Holy Spirit is the third person in the Trinity (Isaiah 48:16; 1 Peter 1:2). And that is also why we see the Holy Spirit known as a "Him" and not "It". Even though the Holy Spirit is Spirit, He is not a ghost!

Many people have a hard time adopting a relationship with the Holy Spirit. They believe in God and know that Jesus has been walking around on earth, but they don't know who the Holy Spirit is. To them, the Holy Spirit is something mysterious or occult, something they cannot grasp because they don't know the Word of God.

We must understand that Jesus spoke about the Holy Spirit as our Helper and our Advocate, as a person that would come and stay with us and teach us all things, just as Jesus had been with the disciples and taught them during the time He walked the earth. This is the season where the Holy Spirit is walking the earth, living inside of all believers.

The Holy Spirit as Spirit

A spirit is a creature without a physical body. When the Bible talks about the Holy Spirit, the words *ruach* and *pneuma* are being used, respectively in Hebrew and Greek. Both parts are names for wind and indicate qualities such as power, strength and ubiquity, that cannot be controlled.

The Holy Spirit is like a wind; it blows wherever it wants. We cannot see Him, but we see the impact of His work - just like the wind moves the leaves in the trees. Still, we cannot predict His next step and tell where He comes from, or where He is going.

The wind blows wherever it pleases. You hear its sound, but you cannot tell where it comes from or where it is going. So it is with everyone born of the Spirit (John 3:8).

In the book of Ezekiel, the Holy Spirit is being compared to a mighty wind, that brings the dead bones back to life.

Then he said to me, "Prophesy to the breath; prophesy, son of man, and say to it, 'This is what the Sovereign Lord says: Come, breath, from the four winds and breathe into these slain, that they may live.'" So I prophesied as he commanded me, and breath entered them; they came to life and stood up on their feet - a vast army (Ezekiel 37:9-10).

The prophet Ezekiel was told to prophesy life to the dead bones and, when it happened, he saw how the bones were being put back together. They rose up and became a mighty army.

It was the Spirit of God who made the whole difference. In the same way, God wants to blow His wind on the church. I have seen how the Holy Spirit can come upon a dead church with revival and create new life in people who are just as dry as Ezekiel's dead bones.

Prophecies of the Holy Spirit

The coming of the Holy Spirit was predicted by the prophets hundreds of years before the birth of Jesus. One of the most known predictions is a prophecy from the book of Joel" that Peter used in his preaching in Jerusalem on the day of Pentecost:

And afterward, I will pour out my Spirit on all people. Your sons and daughters will prophesy, your old men will dream dreams, your young men will see visions. Even on my servants, both men and women, I will pour out my Spirit in those days (Joel 2:28-29).

Isaiah prophesied about how the Holy Spirit was going to be poured out like water upon the dry ground, onto the people of God and their families.

You can also find a prophecy about how He will speak to His people with strange tongues which could be through people of foreign nationalities or through the gift of tongues!

For I will pour water on the thirsty land, and streams on the dry ground; I will pour out my Spirit on your offspring, and my blessing on your descendants" (Isaiah 44:3).

With foreign lips and strange tongues God will speak to this people (Isaiah 28:11).

Isaiah received this prophecy about a strange nation who pronounced words of unknown utterance to the Israelites. Could this prophecy possibly be about God's people, the church, that God wanted to use as a mouthpiece for the message of salvation to Israel today? And the strange words - could that be the language of the Spirit foretold?

In the new Danish translation, the words are explained as "baby language or drunk talk", that shows how the gift of tongues is not to be understood by the natural mind or by Queen Margarethe II of Denmark who approved the translation of the Danish Bible.

In the NET translation, it says that "the Lord's word to them will sound like meaningless gibberish, senseless babbling, a syllable here, a syllable there" which is the prophets way of describing what he heard when he had the vision, it was obviously something he did not understand!

The Holy Spirit Is a Person

The Spirit of God has many names, witnessing to his character and function. The Spirit teaches and instructs us. He gives us good advice and guides us when we need to make important decisions. He awakens our dead spirit and brings it back to life, and when the devil comes with all his accusations, He speaks our case before the throne of God. He is our:

> Teacher (Luke 12:12; 1 John 2:27).
> Adviser (John 14:26; John 15:26; John 16:13).
> Guide (John 16:13; Acts 10:19; Acts 16:6).
> Giver of Life (John 6:63; Romans 8:11; 2 Corinthians 3:6; 1 Peter 3:18).
> Spokesman (John 15:7).

With this comes a number of metaphors that provide a more nuanced picture of the Holy Spirit:

> Our Living Water (John 7:37-38; Ezekiel 47:1-9).
> A Mighty Wind (Acts 2:2; John 3:8).
> Fire (Luke 3:16; Acts 2:3).
> God's Anointing Oil (Acts 10:38; 1 Samuel 16:13).
> A Dove (Matthew 3:16).
> A Seal That Cannot Be Broken (Ephesians 1:13).
> A Pledge Of Our Inheritance (Ephesians 1:14).

The Mission of the Holy Spirit

When Jesus speaks about the Holy Spirit in John 14:16-17, there is no doubt that the Holy Spirit is a person sent from God with a specific mission.

His duties include:
Reminding us of the Word of God (John 14:26).
Witnessing of Christ (John 15:26).
Convicting people of sin (John 16:7-8).
Teaching things we don't understand (John 16:13).
Glorifying Jesus (John 16:14).

It is the Holy Spirit's principal task to make Jesus great! The Holy Spirit holds the character and nature of God. He is not limited by time and place, but is completely perfect in all things.

He is everlasting (Hebrews 9:14).
He is holy in all that He does (Romans 1:4).
We cannot hide from him, because He is omniscient (1 Corinthians 2:10-11).
He is omnipresent (Psalms 139:7-12).
When we feel weak, His power works with mighty strength in us who believe (Ephesians 1:19).

In all of His divinity, the Holy Spirit also has a number of human qualities:

He thinks and understands (1 Corinthians 2:10-11).
He carries sorrow (Ephesians 4:30).
He can feel mocked (Hebrews 10:29).
He can feel pain (Acts 5:3).
He has a will (1 Corinthians 12:11).

He speaks to us (Acts 13:2).

He hinders us from doing certain things (Acts 16:6).

The Holy Spirit in the Old Testament

In the Old Testament, it was the Holy Spirit who hovered over the waters, the surface of the deep, when the world was created. God spoke the Word, and the Holy Spirit brought the Word to life so it manifested and brought it into being.

> *In the beginning God created the heavens and the earth. Now the earth was formless and empty, darkness was over the surface of the deep, and the Spirit of God was hovering over the waters. And God said, "Let there be light," and there was light (Genesis 1:1-3).*

In Jewish history, we read about how the Holy Spirit has helped people throughout the centuries in many different ways:

He was in Joseph so he was able to interpret the dreams at Pharaoh's court (Genesis 41:38). He inspired the craftspeople to build the tabernacle in the desert. (Exodus 31:3). He was there at the selection of Moses' 70 elders (Leviticus 11:17). He gave wisdom to Joshua so he could possess Jericho (Deuteronomy 34:9). He dressed Gideon when he stood in front of his enemies (Judges 6:34). He moved Samson in the town of Ashkelon (Judges 13 and 14). He revealed himself to Ezekiel and made him speak the Word of God to God's people (Ezekiel 11:1). Time after time, He spoke through the prophets and gave kings wisdom, including

King David, who wrote the greater part of the book of Psalms inspired by God's Spirit (2 Samuel 23:2).

Jesus and the Holy Spirit

I already explained how the Holy Spirit played an active role in Jesus' life and ministry:

Jesus was conceived by the Holy Spirit (Luke 1:35).
Jesus was filled with the Holy Spirit (Luke 4:1).
Jesus was led by the Holy Spirit (Matthew 4:1).
Jesus baptized with the Holy Spirit (Luke 3:16).

The Holy Spirit was His Friend and, when Jesus could no longer stay on earth, He made his disciples a promise that the Holy Spirit would come to them in the same way, as it was told by the prophets.

Jesus rejoiced on behalf of the disciples, and was looking forward to seeing the powerful works of the Holy Spirit in their lives. One of the reasons for this was that Jesus couldn't be everywhere at the same time. He was Emmanuel, "God *with* us," as the Holy Spirit is "God *in* us".

In the approximately 30 years Jesus lived on earth, He was physically limited to the country of Israel. However, by the coming of the Holy Spirit, He is now able to be everywhere by His power, to work in *every* believer.

Jesus had a deep relationship with the Holy Spirit and was depending on His guidance in all situations. It should also be the same for you and for me who are called to walk in the footsteps of Jesus.

The Holy Spirit calls us into a deeper life with Him so that we can hear what He says and operate in His power, in the same way Jesus did. It is not just about the supernatural dimension, but about having a relationship with Him, who makes all of His fullness possible within us.

Parakletos

Jesus spoke a lot about the Holy Spirit. He prepared his disciples for the coming of the Holy Spirit, so that they should not be afraid of losing courage the day that He no longer was among them.

The disciples didn't understand why He had to leave them, but Jesus knew that it was necessary. Otherwise, they would not get the Spokesman, He said.

The word spokesman (Greek: *parakletos*) can be translated to the word lawyer or counselor. He is our Defender, Helper and Comforter in hard times, if the accuser rises up against us. When we are judged and put to the test, the Holy Spirit is always ready to give us advice:

And I will ask the Father, and he will give you another Advocate to help you and be with you forever— the Spirit of Truth. The world cannot accept Him, because it neither sees Him nor knows Him. But you know Him, for He lives with you and will be in you (John 14:16-17).

But the Advocate, the Holy Spirit, whom the Father will send in My name, will teach you all things and will remind you of everything I have said to you (John 14:26).

When the Advocate comes, whom I will send to you from the Father—the Spirit of Truth who goes out from the Father—He will testify about Me (John 15:26).

But very truly I tell you, it is for your good that I am going away. Unless I go away, the Advocate will not come to you; but if I go, I will send Him to you (John 16:7-15).

Chapter 8

FOR ALL AGES

Because you are his sons, God sent the Spirit of his Son into our hearts, the Spirit who calls out, "Abba, Father (Galatians 4:6).

On my first crusade in the Faroe Islands, I stood on the platform in the biggest sports arena, not knowing what I was going to preach. As I looked through a few different messages, I suddenly realized that it was the actual day of Pentecost, so what would be more natural than preaching about the baptism of the Holy Spirit?

I preached with boldness and spoke the Word. After that, I invited people to come for prayer. The first five came to the altar, then 10, then 20, then 30, then 40, and so on. Finally, there were about 100 people at the altar who wanted to be filled with the Holy Spirit and power. Everybody stood, staring at me, expecting that I was going to fill their mouths with unintelligible sounds and, again, I had to stress the importance to them that it wasn't me, but God who gives.

Instead of praying for people individually, I released the power of God in the hall. "Be filled," I shouted, but there was no reaction. People just stood and waited like little young birds waiting for heaven to open up and tongues of fire to come sit on their heads. It obviously wasn't going to happen that way.

I was desperate to see God's power released and, when I looked out at the people, my eyes caught a young guy who had received the language of the Spirit the night before. The Holy Spirit showed me I should ask him to come up on the stage. And when I put the microphone in front of him, he immediately started speaking in tongues. This young man's family was known by everybody there so it became a mighty sign for the gathering. Immediately when he started speaking in tongues, it spread to the first row where more and more of the crowd began speaking the language of the Spirit.

The next person I brought to the stage was a little boy. Soon, the stage and the floor was full of young and elderly people praising God in their new tongues. I will never forget seeing a father who was trying to take his little daughter home. When I left the meeting, I saw him walking toward me by himself. I rolled down the window in the car and asked about his daughter. The man told me that he had to leave her on the platform, because she was too drunk (in the Spirit) to walk on her own.

No Age Limit

How old do you have to be in order to get filled with the Holy Spirit? If God is no respecter of persons, then there will be no age limit or censorship on any specific spiritual experiences either. It is not God who created the generation gap in society. With Him, there is no difference between young and old, child and adult.

The Holy Spirit has no age. God uses babies and suckling's mouthes as safeguards, protection (Psalm 8:3) and praise (Matthew 21:16). So it should be fully possible for children to speak in tongues, although they are not "old enough" according to some adults.

How old do you have to be in order to serve Jesus? How old do you have to be in order to praise God? If nature with the ocean, earth and heaven can praise Him, don't you think that human children who are the greatest creation of all can do the same thing?

Jesus says that the Kingdom of God is peace, righteousness and joy in the Holy Spirit. Woe to us if we, as adults, try to prevent children from taking part in the Holy Spirit when Jesus said that our Father in heaven will give the Holy Spirit to all who ask:

> *Which of you fathers, if your son asks for a fish, will give him a snake instead? Or if he asks for an egg, will give him a scorpion? If you then, though you are evil, know how to give good gifts to your children, how much more will your Father in heaven give the Holy Spirit to those who ask Him! (Luke 11:11-13).*

Imagine the most perfect father who has walked here on earth. Jesus is talking about our Father in Heaven as a good Father who gives good gifts to his children. He loves to give us the Holy Spirit. He will not give us a snake when we ask for a fish, or a scorpion when we ask for an egg. You are perfectly safe with Him.

No Spiritual Minors

I meet parents who don't want their children to experience the baptism of the Holy Spirit. They are afraid that their children will be harmed. It's almost as if they are wearing fear on the outside of their clothes and, the worst thing is, it influences the kids.

I don't understand this attitude. Does the Word of God say that the gift of the Holy Spirit is to adults only? No, there ain't no Holy Spirit made "just for adults" or "just for kids." There is no Holy Spirit for Sunday school teachers to go and buy in a toy store. God's children need God's power every day to be able to live life as Christians. It is not easy to be a child or to be young and the developments in society don't make it any easier. Who shall guide them and reveal the truth to them in a world going to hell? God looks affectionately towards children. He's also looks at anyone who tries to keep children away from His heavenly Kingdom. God's Word says there will be judgement for those who cause a believing child to stumble:

> *If anyone causes one of these little ones—those who believe in me—to stumble, it would be better for them to have a large millstone hung around their*

neck and to be drowned in the depths of the sea
(Matthew 18:6).

Our children speak in tongues. Our youngest didn't
say a word in Danish before he was two years old. He
only spoke when he was by himself, laying in his bed
babbling and singing with a joyful smile on his face. I
am convinced that he was praising God in his own way.

We have to understand how children react
unproblematically to the Word of God. They have great
faith. They just believe what they are told.

Samuel, the prophet, grew up in the temple as a
child. He could hear the Voice of God, and he became a
messenger. David was just a young boy when he stood
before Goliath. John, the Baptist, who prepared the way
for Jesus, was chosen to do ministry when he was in his
mother's womb (1 Samuel 3:1; 1 Samuel 17:42; Luke
1:15).

Holy Spirit BBQ
One evening, I was barbecuing together with a dad and
his youngest daughter who was only nine years old.
When we were about to say grace, I started out by
praising God in tongues. I did not think about it but I
noticed the daughter staring at me. Afterwards, I asked
her why she didn't join us in prayer and then I realized I
had stepped into a hurtful zone.

The young girl told how she'd been prayed for
several times but still couldn't speak in tongues.
Disappointment was hanging over her like a cloud and

the father tried to comfort her, saying that it would happen at the summer camp they were about to attend one month later. It was almost like hearing myself before I got baptized with the Holy Spirit!

I know by experience that the Holy Spirit comes when the heart is ready, whether you call on Him in the Sunday service at church, at the summer festival or around the fire in the backyard making smores on a normal Tuesday evening.

An entire month is a long time to wait especially for a little girl. I encouraged her and told her that tonight was her night. As she ran inside to get her Bible, I was left with her concerned father. He thought it was a terrible thing that I'd promised his daughter the Holy Spirit after being prayed for so many times without any positive result. He was afraid that she would not receive it and end up feeling like a failure.

I just took it easy and started teaching the girl in the Word of God with the father, on the other hand, wishing and hoping that his daughter wasn't going to leave disappointed again. As we went through the last Scriptures, I saw tears streaming down her cheeks.

"Can I please have the Holy Spirit now?" she asked and, of course, she could.

We went up the hill behind the farm and there, on the most beautiful summer night, she was praising God in new tongues like it was the most natural thing in the world for her to do. Her father was crying tears of happiness. Later in the evening when the older sister came home, she also received the power of God and the gift of speaking in tongues.

Simple and Easy
God wants to reveal Himself to His children, and, therefore, He wishes for all of us to become like children so that we can take part in all that He has given us. He will not hold anything back from his babes:

> At that time Jesus, full of joy through the Holy Spirit, said, "I praise you, Father, Lord of heaven and earth, because you have hidden these things from the wise and learned, and revealed them to little children. Yes, Father, for this is what you were pleased to do (Luke 10:21).

If the Holy Spirit fell on every single person on the day of Pentecost and in the book of Acts, don't you think that the children also received their part? Jesus says that the pure of heart shall see God. Who are the pure of heart if not a little child? The Word of God says that children are the greatest in the Kingdom of Heaven.

> At that time the disciples came to Jesus and asked, "Who, then, is the greatest in the kingdom of heaven?" He called a little child to Him, and placed the child among them. And he said: "Truly I tell you, unless you change and become like little children, you will never enter the kingdom of heaven (Matthew 18:1-3).

Children always gathered around Jesus - sometimes so many the disciples were annoyed by it and tried to remove them from Him. But Jesus did not try to get them away. Instead, He said that the little ones should come to Him:

> *Then people brought little children to Jesus for him to place his hands on them and pray for them. But the disciples rebuked them. Jesus said, "Let the little children come to Me, and do not hinder them, for the kingdom of heaven belongs to such as these (Matthew 19:13-14).*

Children are very sensitive toward the Spirit of God. I have seen kids speak in tongues, prophesy, heal the sick, and cast out demons with greater faith and boldness than many adults. My oldest boy was just five years old when he went around during intercession in one of our revival meetings, prophesying to the adults until they fell on their knees, hit by the power of God. I had not asked him to do it. He did it on his own initiative!

We are the Heirs

God made us his children by the new birth, so why shouldn't children be able to receive the gift of the Holy Spirit?

> *For those who are led by the Spirit of God are the children of God. The Spirit you received does not make you slaves, so that you live in fear again; rather, the Spirit you received brought about your adoption to sonship. And by him we cry, "Abba, Father." The Spirit himself testifies with our spirit that we are God's children (Romans 8:14-16).*

When we look at children, it's easier for us to understand our relationship to our Father in Heaven: To be a child is not a question of age, but about family and belonging. My children have a special status in my life. When they were younger I made sure they had food, clothes to wear and money in their bank account. My children are loved no matter how they act and, if they act incorrectly, I will teach and correct them. By that I show them that they are my children, for other children I do not freely correct.

And have you completely forgotten this word of encouragement that addresses you as a father addresses his son? It says, "My son, do not make light of the Lord's discipline, and do not lose heart when he rebukes you, because the Lord disciplines the one he loves, and he chastens everyone he accepts as his son." Endure hardship as discipline; God is treating you as his children. For what children are not disciplined by their father? (Hebrews 12:5-7).

If the Spirit of God lives in you, you are a child of God no matter how old you are. The chastening that you go through is proof that you are full member of God's worldwide family with all the privileges it provides, including the right to inherit all the heavenly glory.

Now if we are children, then we are heirs - heirs of God and co-heirs with Christ, if indeed we share in his sufferings in order that we may also share in his glory (Romans 8:17).

The Word of God says that the righteous man will leave an inheritance for the generations to come (Proverbs 13:22). God will care for us in the same way. There is an inheritance in Heaven that's waiting for us, and that we shall not doubt. He has given us the Holy Spirit as a promise for this inheritance to come (Ephesians 1:13). What a wonderful Father in Heaven we have!

As a parent, you should teach your children about the language of the Holy Spirit and teach them to use it in the same way you have learned and taught them about the salvation of Jesus Christ. Tell them about their heavenly inheritance! Why should they only hear the Christmas story of baby Jesus in a manger, or even the Easter message of Jesus on the cross and the empty grave? Why not also teach them about the tongues at Pentecost so they can live to the fullest by the power of the Holy Spirit?

Chapter 9

WHY SPEAK IN TONGUES?

But you, dear friends, by building yourselves up in your most holy faith and praying in the Holy Spirit (Jude 1:20).

When God wants to give the Holy Spirit and the gift of speaking in tongues as a sign, it is for a reason. It is not just to have the gift of speaking in tongues sitting "on the shelf." God wants you to *use* the gift. If you don't use it, it will slowly die out - just like it happens with a foreign language that we once learned in school but never really used.

My wife had that problem when we first met. If you asked her if she spoke in tongues, she'd say "yes," Speaking in tongues was like a trophy, a witness of something she'd been hunting for once but was very well hidden and rarely used. She didn't quite understand the necessity of speaking in tongues and, therefore, had not used the gift for many years. At one point, she almost had to start all over again, asking God for forgiveness for having neglected to use the gift that He had given her. Then, the breakthrough she was seeking was given!

Many Christians, who have been filled with the Holy Ghost have lost the gift of speaking in tongues because they haven't been practicing their spiritual language. They have never understood why it is necessary. Personally, I only need one explanation: it is biblical. I want to take part in all the blessings that are found in the Word of God!

The Spirit Equips
When God sent the Holy Spirit to the disciples, it was not to sit in a charismatic meeting and speak secrets with God in code language. The intention was not to be inward, but to be outward. The Holy Spirit came to equip them so they could go into the streets and testify of the resurrected Jesus, which they needed the power of God to do. It was He who gave them boldness and made them witnesses, and it was He who gave them power to work with their spiritual gifts.

After the day of Pentecost (Acts 2), we see the change in Chapter 3 found in the story of the lame man by the gate of the temple called Beautiful.

One day Peter and John were going up to the temple at the time of prayer—at three in the afternoon. Now a man who was lame from birth was being carried to the temple gate called Beautiful, where he was put every day to beg from those going into the temple courts. When he saw Peter and John about to enter, he asked them for money. Peter looked straight at him, as did John. Then Peter said, "Look at us!" So the man gave them his attention, expecting to get something from them. Then Peter said, "Silver or gold I do not have, but what I do have I give you. In the name of Jesus Christ of Nazareth, walk." Taking him by the right hand, he helped him up, and instantly the man's feet and ankles became strong. He jumped to his feet and began to walk. Then he went with them into the temple courts, walking and jumping, and praising God (Acts 3:1-8).

Imagine how many times Peter and John had been walking by this lame man without healing him. Now, walking by him again, things were different. Instead of just passing by, they grabbed the man by his hand and commanded him to rise up and walk which he did immediately.

What was the difference? It is obvious they had received the "power to become" (Acts 1:8). The power of God had equipped them, and "signs and wonders" had begun to follow them.

We see how both of them had received a new sensitivity toward the Spirit of God, so that they could hear what the Spirit wanted them to do. The love of God was poured out into their hearts by the Holy Spirit (Romans 5:5). With faith active in love (Galatians 5:6), the Spirit of God did not allow them to pass by the man without meeting his needs.

The Spirit Edifies

When we speak in tongues we strengthen our spiritual man. The expression "edify" is the Greek word *epoikodomeo*, which means to build with stones on a foundation which has already been made. What an amazing metaphor! God is edifying our spirits as we speak in tongues, building on the foundation of salvation in Christ.

Anyone who speaks in a tongue edifies themselves (1 Corinthians 14:4).

In some translations, it says the one who speaks in tongues *only* builds up himself. The word "only" has been used negatively as an excuse for not speaking in tongues. It is wrong to devalue the meaning of personal edification. We must edify ourselves before we can edify the church. Together we shall grow in maturity where we can contain the fullness of Christ.

The word *edify* could be substituted for the word *recharge*. Our spirit is like a battery that needs recharging by the Holy Spirit; if you want the faith engine to run you should use the gift of tongues continuously by always praying in the Spirit.

Personal edification and prayer *in* the Holy Spirit (Jude 20) should not be confused with prayer *led* by the Spirit. When you pray in the Spirit, in tongues, the mind is without fruit (1 Corinthians 14:15). Praying in the Spirit cannot be understood with the human mind. Prayer led by the Spirit is different. They are words inspired by the Holy Spirit spoken in your native language.

The Spirit Teaches

When I was baptized with the Holy Spirit, I got a lot more sensitive to the direction of the Spirit of God. Suddenly, there were things I could not do because the Holy Spirit reminded me it was wrong. But there were also things I could do with great joy, like praying and reading the Bible. They were no longer law, but a desire.

To speak in tongues is like plugging a lamp into the wall; turn on the power and the light will shine. When the power button is switched on, we can testify of Him with signs, wonders and miracles. If the connection isn't good, the power will never flow through our lives.

When you begin to speak in tongues, access is granted in the realm of the supernatural. The natural mind does not have understanding of that which is from God. This is where we need the Holy Spirit to help. He brings words taught by the Spirit (aka the language of the Spirit), which brings revelation of what God has given us by grace:

What we have received is not the spirit of the world, but the Spirit who is from God, so that we may understand what God has freely given us. This is what we speak, not in words taught us by human wisdom but in words taught by the Spirit, explaining spiritual realities with Spirit-taught words (1 Corinthians 2:12-13).

When I pray, it often happens that I receive knowledge and insight into the lives of others. People wonder and ask how that can be, but it's actually really simple. I get my inspiration from the Holy Spirit. When I speak in tongues, the Holy Spirit gives me words from God. He sends his streams of living water and speaking in tongues is the bucket with which I draw up the water (Proverbs 18:1, Proverbs 21:2).

The same passage tells of the secret wisdom of God which is revealed to us by the Holy Spirit. A person does not possess all wisdom of the world. If all wisdom of the world was a layered cake and I was to cut a piece to show how wise I was, I would not even dare to lift the knife.

I only know a little but the Holy Spirit knows everything. He has deep insight into everything that is found with God. He doesn't just search our hearts. He searches the depths of God.

Imagine the Holy Spirit coming with a search warrant, knocking on the doors of our hearts. He has the permission to search our inner man, check out all corners and turn everything upside down.

As you are praying in the Holy Spirit, He will highlight things that you have not known about yourself. He will reveal hidden thoughts of your heart and lead you to repentance so you can receive God's amazing grace.

Intercession for God's People

Another side of speaking in tongues is intercession for the saints, your brothers and sisters in Christ. The gift of tongues is the four-wheel drive in your prayer life. When you pray, you can change between tongues and your native language. You can pray in the Spirit and with your intellect and you will experience how the Spirit intercedes when you can't find the right words yourself:

> *In the same way, the Spirit helps us in our weakness. We do not know what we ought to pray for, but the Spirit himself intercedes for us through wordless groans. And he who searches our hearts knows the mind of the Spirit, because the Spirit intercedes for God's people in accordance with the will of God (Romans 8:26-27).*

It has always fascinated me when speaking in tongues, you speak secrets with God. Tongues is like a code language that Satan does not understand!

When we pray in tongues, we never have to be afraid to ask for something that is not God's will. The Spirit helps us in our weakness. The Holy Spirit in us expresses God's will and intercedes when our words comes to an end. We often don't know what to pray or how we should pray. But God has given us the gift of tongues as a tool to pray through the issue or circumstance.

The Bible teaches us that we should pray without ceasing (1 Thessalonians 5:17, Jude 1: 20). Most of us would run out of words praying in our natural language within a minute or two. We cannot pray without ceasing with our own intellect/minds, but we can pray in the Spirit while our minds are at rest, both day and night!

There is a dynamic fellowship with the Holy Spirit where direct guidance is crucial, an important spice to a life lived in continuous transformation. I thank God for having given us the gift of tongues. It is simply genius, being able to speak in tongues. In this way we can always pray according to the will of God. It does not mean that we should always pray in tongues but, through prayer in the Spirit, we can become inspired to express human words led by the Spirit, so that other people during corporate prayer in church can say 'amen' to our prayer as well.

Joy and Thanksgiving
Rejoice always, pray continually, give thanks in all circumstances; for this is God's will for you in Christ Jesus (1 Thessalonians 5:16-18).

To speak in tongues will make you happy and lighthearted! It is like soda, bubbling inside, making all the heaviness bubble away.

Scripture says we should always be joyful. How is that possible? Read it again and you will find the answer in the next sentence: Never stop praying and be thankful in all circumstances. This is the secret to a powerful Christian life.

In the natural, it can sometimes be hard to give thanks, but the Holy Spirit in us always thanks God for all He has done. You will see how tongues and thankfulness goes together, like a set of pedals going up and down making the wheels spin around. By speaking in tongues, our thanksgiving goes up to God and when we are thankful we cannot stop speaking in tongues. What a wonderful interaction!

Stop for a moment and think about all that God has given or done for you. There is so much to be grateful for. We are His children. We are saved by His grace. We have all in Him. He is our life. He loves us with an everlasting love. He cares for us in all things. He has not left us helpless, but has freely given us the Holy Spirit to stay with us forever.

When we come together as the people of God, we have an incredible amount for which to be thankful from Him. That is why it is so natural to pray in tongues during prayer and worship. Our hearts overflow with wonderful words. There is nothing better than praising Jesus in tongues, hour after hour and, as you are doing this, you can even experience how God will give you new songs and melodies. This should be a natural thing as we come together and worship. Why do you think the Psalms talk about singing a *new* song unto the Lord?

Prayer is many things.You can sit quietly. You can jump and dance and shout for joy, cry and wait for the Spirit. When you step into this spiritual dimension, hours fly by. Did you know that you were created to worship? Your spirit-man longs for this kind of intimate fellowship with God's Holy Spirit but, to come to that point, you must be willing to lay everything down before Him.

The spirit man is like a bird in a cage caught behind the bars of the soul longing to break out into freedom. But there is a "window" to the heavenly we can open ourselves to when we speak the language of the Spirit - from the depths of our hearts to the depths of God's heart.

The Spirit Sets Us Free

In the beginning of our ministry, we were facilitating several rehab centers for drug addicts, alcoholics and other people in need. When we took people into the program, the first thing we would do was to pray with them to receive the baptism of the Holy Spirit. After this, we would take them through three days of prayer and fasting as they were being delivered from evil spirits. We were praying over them night and day. We experienced how the gift of tongues helped them through, setting them free from any symptoms, including withdrawal.

The Holy Spirit would lead us to take authority over the dark and demonic powers in their lives. Old ways of thinking and walls would be broken down; the Holy Spirit would reveal things from their past through words of knowledge and prophecy. This would establish confession of sin, forgiveness and healing of deep wounds from the past.

The Holy Spirit is our Helper. He is the Spirit of Truth, demolishing all the lies. He is the One who guides us to the whole truth, so that we can know the truth and walk into the freedom that God has for all of us.

Then you will know the truth, and the truth will set you free (John 8:32).

The most powerful way to overcome any kind of addiction is to fight back in the Spirit with the Word of God, speaking in tongues and praying. We have seen all kinds of addicts delivered through prayer and fasting. The more they spoke in tongues, the stronger they became.

Did Tongues Cease?
There is a lot of good reasons to speak in tongues, you don't have to know them all but, when it is in the Bible, why not go all in?

I have met church people who believe tongues are not for us today; that the gift of tongues died out with the apostles (referring to 1 Corinthians 13:9-10 where Paul teaches about "that which is perfect"). These church people are reading the Bible with the wrong glasses. Paul is referring to spending eternity with Jesus; when this happens, we will not need the gifts of the Spirit anymore!

If the spiritual gifts died out with the apostles, how can Paul instruct the church in Rome about prophecy which is one of the nine spiritual gifts? We see how they were prophesying, even though none of the apostles had ever been in Rome!

We have different gifts, according to the grace given to each of us. If your gift is prophesying, then prophesy in accordance with your faith (Romans 12:6).

The gift of prophecy did not die out with the apostles. Neither did the gift of tongues! The Holy Spirit is still around; this is an historical fact. Throughout church history, God has poured out his Spirit and the revival that we experience today is a result of this outpouring.

We live in the end times, where God has promised us the greatest revival ever in history. How are people going to be awakened if there are no supernatural manifestations present? As the first believers were living out the book of Acts, we should do the same, writing new chapters every day, experiencing the outpour of the Holy Spirit and His power on a daily basis.

It was not only the apostles who were anointed to pass on the power of the Holy Spirit. If that was the case, then why would Paul teach the Romans about speaking in tongues? Why would he teach on the gift of prophecy and the other gifts that works together with the gift of tongues (Romans 12:6)? And why would he say that the gifts of God are irrevocable (Romans 11:29) if the gifts were being withdrawn? We see how the gifts were being passed through prophecy and the laying of hands by the elders to young Timothy, the next generation of believers:

> *Do not neglect your gift, which was given you through prophecy when the body of elders laid their hands on you (1 Timothy 4:14).*

Why would God consider giving gifts to the early church and not for us today?

> *For God's gifts and his call are irrevocable (Romans 11:29).*

Chapter 10

STRIVE FOR THE GIFTS

Now eagerly desire the greater gifts. And yet I will show you the most excellent way (1 Corinthians 12:31).

Paul teaches us to strive for the gifts. We should be eager to get them, not just sitting and waiting for them to come! Maybe you don't like this expression but it is alright to be a "climber" in the Kingdom of God, done with modesty.

When it comes to spiritual gifts, we cannot go by our polite and cautious nature. The word *strive* is the Greek word *zeloo*, which means to be fired up, or on fire for something.

This is more than just a birthday wish. This is to desire it earnestly with all of your heart. To strive for the gift is to be one hundred percent occupied by this one goal, making a great deal of effort not to reject what you long for.

The word *zeloo*, freely translated, would be to jump in front of the line. The expression contains great zealousness, jealousy and a good portion of a competitive spirit where one desires it so much that one does not shy away from receiving it.

These feelings many have been taught to suppress and consider to be negative. According to the Ten Commandments, we are not to desire our neighbor's spouse or estate, but when we talk about spiritual gifts it's okay to press in. We must come to a point where we understand God's thoughts on spiritual gifts.

Tongues is not something for which we strive, for personal gain. It certainly is for personal edification, but it will always be for the benefit of others. Just imagine what impact it would have in the congregation on a Sunday morning if everybody would spend time with the Holy Spirit and edify themselves before going to church!

Different Spiritual Gifts
We are called to be united, to be "one in the Spirit." We often see the opposite. People in the church discuss spiritual gifts and denominations are born. The word, denomination, means "divided people." It is made by man and is definetly not the description we will find in Scripture.

The church is the body of Christ and He is the head of the church which consists of many different body parts each with their own special function and gifting (1 Corinthians 12:4-11).

The distribution and significance of spiritual gifts are explained using the illustration of one body and different body parts. Something tells us that the Corinthians pointed out some spiritual gifts were more important than others. It seems like there were problems in those days with divisions within the church. The gifts are different and, depending on the gift God has given to you, there will always be different views along the way. Paul urged the church in Corinth to hold on to the unity of the Spirit exactly in this situation. No one should boast on behalf of others for there is not to be strife (verses 12-27).

The chapter ends with a resume of the different ministry gifts within the church: apostles, prophets and teachers. The spiritual gifts tie themselves to these different ministries. As a minister, you might not have all the gifts but, together in the church, we have them all.

Unlimited Riches

God is more than enough for all who call on His name. When it comes to spiritual gifts, I have met great men and women of God who are in possession of all nine of the spiritual gifts mentioned in God's Word. That tells me we should strive for as many of them as possible, instead of just being content with just a few.

If God has served us a spiritual "buffet," we should eat and not hold back. There is no limit to how much we can get! If there is an overflow of the gifts, then we shouldn't be content with just two of them. We should never limit God.

Striving is not a suggestion, but an instruction! Even though we all have different ministries/body parts, Paul still asks if everyone can speak in tongues, interpret tongues, heal the sick and so on. I used to think that the answer was "no" just because we have not seen it. But what if the answer is "yes?" God is bigger than our limited understanding. He is an "out of the box" God. Let's always grow in revelation and recognition of our unlimited God.

There has been a lot of confusion about spiritual gifts. Many books have been published on the subject, including books with a devised system which is supposed to help Christians find out what gifts they have and those they do not have.

Most people have the gift of helping, the gift to give, the gift to love and so on, while only a few people have the more supernatural gifts such as the gift of healing. Some people claim that they have the gift of discerning spirits but they do not cast them out. Instead they use their "gift" to criticize their Christian brothers and sisters.

A book on gift discovering will not give you the answer. There is a lot of confusion in this area in the church because people focus on talents and abilities instead of focusing on God and what He can give.

If we don't change our focus, we deceive ourselves. I have met Christians who tell me they have the gift of healing the sick even though they have never prayed for a sick person. I wonder how they came to that conclusion?

If you have a spiritual gift, then use it and let your life speak instead of your words. The spiritual gifts talk about God, not you. When God gives, it's not for us to keep for ourselves. If you have the gift of healing, you communicate that to those who are sick. If you have the gift of prophesy, you prophesy a word of exhortation, edification and/or comfort. Your particular gifting doesn't show through a test on spiritual gifts; it becomes visible the day you start to put it into practice.

The Will of the Spirit
You don't have to pray and fast to ask God if it is His will to receive the impartation of spiritual gifts. Just read the Word. If God already said we should strive, then it would be disobedient not to do what God has said.

God's opponent, satan, will tell you to relax and stay content the way you are. If he can stop you from expressing your spiritual gifts, he can control the situation. But, as soon as people are baptized with the Holy Spirit, a snowball effect occurs. A whole new world of signs, wonders and miracles opens up as they begin to exercise their spiritual authority.

Satan knows the Bible. He knows that the Kingdom of God does not only consist of words of wisdom, but in the evidence of the Spirit and power (1 Corinthians 4:20, 2:4; 1 Thessalonians 1:5; Acts 10:38). That's why he always tries to suck the power out of the gospel by creating disagreements about spiritual gifts.

The more discussion, the harder it gets for an individual to receive what comes from God. But remember, the Spirit shares the spiritual gifts with whomever He wants (1 Corinthians 12:11). Some people resign when they hear this and might think "Your will be done" – but, if you put on the glasses of faith, you will see it says that the Spirit *wants* to. This is the will of the Spirit! You should not lack any spiritual gifts. God's Word says that you should strive to get it! When you understand this, God will give you a new boldness. Now you can start to receive from the Spirit, to live in the Spirit and follow the holy impulses the Spirit gives you.

This is the confidence we have in approaching God: That if we ask anything according to His will, He hears us (1 John 5:14).

Invade Heaven
Even though the disciples were waiting for 40 days to be empowered from on high, you don't need to wait any longer. It is time to push! Maybe you learned that the Holy Spirit is a gentleman who doesn't push, but it is the same Holy Spirit who comes like a mighty wind and blows you out of your shoes!

God wants for all to be filled with the power of the Holy Spirit. He is waiting for you to lean back and enjoy the ride. Don't let fear hold you back from jumping on the train. Far too many Christians are in a waiting position concerning spiritual gifts because they don't feel worthy. False humility will leave you empty-handed. God wants to equip all of His saints. It is those who take it by force who get to take part in it.

From the days of John the Baptist until now, the kingdom of heaven has been subjected to violence, and violent people have been raiding it (Matthew 11:12).

If you hunger and thirst for the Holy Spirit in your life, you are fully qualified to receive what you ask for. Hunger generates desperation and creates results. Therefore, God loves the hungry above those who feel like they have enough:

He has filled the hungry with good things but has sent the rich away empty (Luke 1:53).

When I first got saved I led a Muslim friend to the Lord. When he heard about the gift of prophecy, he decided to pursue this gift. He read the Bible nonstop - morning, noon and evening. He slept with his Bible under his pillow and got up in the middle of the night to read. He prayed with a zeal I have rarely seen. Two weeks after he got saved, he received his first prophetic message and, right after that, he spoke fluently in tongues. Due to his great zeal, he received both the gifts of prophesy and tongues at the same time. He had only been saved for two weeks!

I know Christians who have been saved for 20 years and still struggle to find out what spiritual gifts they have, still wondering if the spiritual language they received 15 years ago by laying on of hands really was from God! Remember, God will not give you a stone when you ask for bread. If you have asked for the Holy Spirit, don't you think that is what you will receive?

I heard about a Korean pastor who told how the members of his ministry were prophesying and receiving words of knowledge as soon as they were baptized with the Holy Spirit. "Tongues are a secondary thing," he said. Let's strive after the gifts. Let us not limit God.

A Free Gift
If you get baptized with the Holy Spirit when you feel like you're ready, you never will be ready. God gives His good gifts by grace to all who believe. The truth is: you and I never will be good enough. The only one who is good is our Father in Heaven. Because of His great love, every day in Heaven is like Christmas. When we ask God for the Holy Spirit, He gives it to us. And we get the real deal, not a copy, with the gift of tongues as a sign. You don't have to be afraid because He would never want to give us something that could hurt or harm us. Only good gifts come from God. God gives us the Holy Spirit without conditions.

God does not give according to our abilities, talents or good deeds, but He rewards those who seek Him in spirit and truth (Hebrews 11:6), meaning with a pure heart. Everything is visible to Him, so you might as well just be honest about everything. He knows you're not perfect. If you want to take part in spiritual gifts, you need to understand the word, grace (Greek: charisma), meaning undeserved love.

The gifts of the Holy Spirit are free and they come without conditions. All gifts are obtained exclusively by grace. They do not witness of the receiver (you), but of the giver (God), who descended from heaven and gave Himself as the complete sacrifice for an incomplete world.

This is why it says: "When he ascended on high, he took many captives and gave gifts to his people (Ephesians 4:8).

Every good and perfect gift is from above, coming down from the Father of the heavenly lights, who does not change like shifting shadows (James 1:17).

And hope does not put us to shame, because God's love has been poured out into our hearts through the Holy Spirit, who has been given to us (Romans 5:5).

Our Father in heaven is a giver. He loved the world so much that he first and foremost gave His only Son, and thereafter He gave us the gift of the Holy Spirit, which is the promise of the inheritance that awaits us in heaven. God is a good Father and He loves to spoil His kids!

Greatest of All
As we study the gifts of the Holy Spirit, we end up in 1 Corinthians 13 where the apostle Paul uses an entire

chapter to describe the power of love together with the gift of tongues and other spiritual gifts.

When it says that the greatest gift is love, some Bible scholars use this chapter to prove the gift of tongues and the prophetic gifting don't have any value. But that's not what it says. It is true that love is the greatest of the gifts, but that doesn't mean the gifts of the Spirit should be underestimated. It's not an 'either/ or' situation, but both are included. The one (love) we should do, and the other (spiritual giftings) we need not neglect.

Without love, there is a potential danger that we, in our eagerness to receive spiritual gifts, will get away from the truth just like the false prophets who came to Jesus wearing sheepskin. They looked like the rest of the group but, inside, they were ravenous wolves, focusing on manifestations rather than love for people.

> *Not everyone who says to me, 'Lord, Lord,' will enter the kingdom of heaven, but only the one who does the will of my Father who is in heaven. Many will say to me on that day, 'Lord, Lord, did we not prophesy in your name and in your name drive out demons and in your name perform many miracles?' Then I will tell them plainly, 'I never knew you. Away from me, you evildoers! (Matthew 7:21-23).*

The purpose of this Scripture is not to stop us from doing the supernatural stuff, this passage should rather be a warning for all of us not to be deceived. There are people who prophesy, cast out demons and heal the sick who Jesus claims not to know. That is why love must always be the brand:

> *By this everyone will know that you are my disciples, if you love one another (John 13:35).*

Agape Love

Once a year, I travel to Africa to participate in a huge crusade with my spiritual covering who is a world-renowned evangelist. She preaches to multitudes and meets with ministers and presidents. In spite of this publicity, she has always managed to show love for every individual she meets. I have seen her call forth people suffering from Aids, ministering to them one by one. They had open, oozing wounds all over their bodies, but she was not afraid of their wounds. She hugged them all, even though she exposed herself to infected blood.

The Word of God teaches us that faith is active in love.

> *For in Christ Jesus, neither circumcision nor uncircumcision has any value. All that matters is faith, expressed through love (Galatians 5:6).*

Love is not a feeling, but an action, going that extra mile and reaching out to people in need. It is more than a bond between a man and his wife. It is deeper than love between parents and their children and it is definitely more than the love you can have for a certain television program or your favorite restaurant. We are talking about God's unselfish agape love:

Love is patient, love is kind. It does not envy, it does not boast, it is not proud. It does not dishonor others, it is not self-seeking, it is not easily angered, it keeps no record of wrongs. Love does not delight in evil but rejoices with the truth. It always protects, always trusts, always hopes, always perseveres. Love never fails (1 Corinthians 13:4-8).

We see how Paul laid a good, solid foundation by placing the love chapter in the center of his teaching on "using the gifts of the Spirit" in the early church. If we can keep this love toward God and man, having faith in the gifts of the Spirit and our living Hope of Heaven who awaits us, we cannot avoid getting hold of the real deal.

Chapter 11

INTERPRETATION OR NOT?

There are different kinds of gifts, but the same Spirit distributes them (1 Corinthians 12:4).

The Holy Spirit's job is to make the church ready by preparing the body of Christ for the end of times, before Jesus returns. He does this in two ways: by giving the baptism of the Holy Spirit to the individual and giving the gifts of the Spirit to the church.

There are nine gifts of the Spirit in total:
1. The gift of wisdom: The ability to know the mind of the Holy Spirit and to receive insight into how knowledge may be applied to specific needs.
2. Knowledge: Supernatural insight to know what God is currently doing or intends to do in the life of another person. A form of revelation similar to prophecy or a type of discernment.

3. Faith: The gift to speak and do the impossible, extraordinary confidence in God's promises, power, and presence.
4. Working of miracles: When the Holy Spirit in you works through you to operate outside the bounds of what is natural. Divine manifestations similar to limbs growing out.
5. Gifts of healings: Supernatural enablements given to a believer to minister various kinds of healing and restoration to individuals through the power of the Holy Spirit.
6. Prophecy: The word of God for admonition, edification and comfort.
7. Discernment: To expose demons and false teachings.
8. Tongues: The language of the Holy Spirit spoken to edify the individual.
9. Interpretation of tongues: Works with the gift of speaking in tongues and the gift of prophecy in order to edify the church.

The church in Corinth consisted of people who were active in all nine gifts. There is a whole list to be explored. However, I am not going into details about them all. I will focus instead on the two at the end of this list, the language of the Spirit which is tongues, and the interpretation of tongues.

If you don't know the difference between these two kinds of tongues, you will never understand what Paul is trying to pass on. Some people read with the wrong glasses, inspired by Bible scholars who have never experienced the baptism of the Holy Spirit. In this matter, they are like blind men leading other blind men; they try to comprehend spiritual gifts, not recognizing the fact that the natural mind never will understand matters of the Spirit.

Two Kinds of Tongues

We all have different church cultures. Some church people speak openly in tongues. Some don't. So, who is right? Everybody wants order but, on the other hand, we don't want to quench the Spirit! Would it be okay if some Christians sit and pray quietly in tongues in church during prayer and worship? Should we tell them to be quiet or should we demand a translation?

Paul says that we may not hinder anyone in speaking in tongues (1 Corinthians 14:39). You can easily be in church, speaking quietly to God for yourself (1 Corinthians 14:28). This is between you and God. You have your personal prayer language which is for personal edification and, therefore, does not need interpretation. This type of prayer language is contrary to the public tongue which is for the edification of the church and, therefore, demands a translation.

With this in mind you will see that there is a difference between the two kinds of tongues - as well as how and when to use them.

Follow the way of love and eagerly desire gifts of the Spirit, especially prophecy. For anyone who speaks in a tongue does not speak to people but to God. Indeed, no one understands them; they utter mysteries by the Spirit. But the one who prophesies speaks to people for their strengthening, encouraging and comfort. Anyone who speaks in a tongue edifies themselves, but the one who prophesies edifies the church. I would like every one of you to speak in tongues, but I would rather have you prophesy. The one who prophesies is greater than the one who speaks in tongues, unless someone interprets, so that the church may be edified (1 Corinthians 14:1-5).

In your personal prayer language, you speak secrets with God (verse 2) but, when you prophecy, you edify the church (verse 3). The difference between the two types of prayer languages is that the one who speaks in tongues edifies himself, while the public tongue that is translated edifies, exhorts and comforts the church (verse 4).

Both tongues are okay. Paul encourages the church to both speak in tongues personally and prophetically in the church. If one kinds of tongue should be preferred over the other, it would be the prophetic because it benefits more people; the message is being interpreted so that the church can be edified (verse 5).

Public Tongue
It seems like the church in Corinth would have an overflow of these spiritual gifts, so Paul has to teach them not to preach in tongues in public. Just imagine how would it be if your pastor stood up in church one Sunday and started preaching in tongues instead of preaching the Word in English? It wouldn't make any sense to you!

Now, brothers and sisters, if I come to you and speak in tongues, what good will I be to you, unless I bring you some revelation or knowledge or prophecy or word of instruction? Even in the case of lifeless things that make sounds, such as the pipe or harp, how will anyone know what tune is being played unless there is a distinction in the notes? Again, if the trumpet does not sound a clear call, who will get ready for battle? So it is with you. Unless you speak intelligible words with your tongue, how will anyone know what you are saying? You will just be speaking into the air. Undoubtedly there are all sorts of languages in the world, yet none of them is without meaning. If then I do not grasp the meaning of what someone is saying, I am a foreigner to the speaker, and the speaker is a foreigner to me. So it is with you. Since you are eager for gifts of the Spirit, try to excel in those that build up the church (1 Corinthians 14:6-12).

The church in Corinth experimented with this, but Paul makes them aware that there is no benefit to such preaching (verse 6). He compares a service like this with a trumpet making an uncertain sound which is not able to gather an army for battle (verses 7-8). This is about the way of doing church; if they were so zealous to use the gifts of the Spirit, they should do it well instead of preaching words from the pulpit that no one understands.

Paul is using the gift of discernment. There are many different kinds of spiritual experiences which feel good and gives goose bumps. But, if these experiences do not benefit the church, then it is completely in vain (verses 9-12).

Interpretation or Not?
We don't need to put restrictions on how to worship God. Where the Spirit of the Lord is, there will always be freedom, both to speak in tongues and to interpret tongues, to sing in the Spirit and to sing in English and other languages:

> *For this reason the one who speaks in a tongue should pray that they may interpret what they say. For if I pray in a tongue, my spirit prays, but my mind is unfruitful. So what shall I do? I will pray with my spirit, but I will also pray with my understanding; I will sing with my spirit, but I will also sing with my understanding. Otherwise when you are praising God in the Spirit, how can someone else, who is now put in the position of an inquirer, say "Amen" to your thanksgiving, since they do not know what you are saying? You are giving thanks well enough, but no one else is edified (1 Corinthians 14:13-17).*

When Paul says that he who speaks in tongues should ask God for an interpretation, again, he is referring to the public tongue in the church (verse 13). The same is be recommended during prayer. For example, in prayer meetings, where everybody is praying in tongues without putting words that can be understood to the prayer, the mind stays unfruitful, which means that it does not settle in our souls where our mind, will and emotions live (verse 14). The balance is to do both. Pray in the spiritual language to plug into the Spirit of God and pray out in an understandable language, so that people can say "Amen" to your prayer. Same thing in worship. You can sing in the Spirit (in tongues) but you can also sing psalms and worship the Lord (verse 15). The order should be clear so that those who come from outside the church can come and participate and still understand what is going on (verses 13-17).

God is Truly Among You

Paul's concern is to teach on how speaking in tongues is to be conducted in the church so that people will see how God is present among them. He himself speaks more in tongues than all his church members. He is not concerned that tongues will scare people away. He just wants to make sure that somebody can interpret what is going on!

> *I thank God that I speak in tongues more than all of you. But in the church I would rather speak five intelligible words to instruct others than ten thousand words in a tongue. Brothers and sisters, stop thinking like children. In regard to evil be infants, but in your thinking be adults. In the Law it is written: "With other tongues and through the lips of foreigners I will speak to this people, but even then they will not listen to me, says the Lord." Tongues, then, are a sign, not for believers but for unbelievers; prophecy, however, is not for unbelievers but for believers. So if the whole church comes together and everyone speaks in tongues, and inquirers or unbelievers come in, will they not say*

that you are out of your mind? But if an unbeliever or an inquirer comes in while everyone is prophesying, they are convicted of sin and are brought under judgment by all, as the secrets of their hearts are laid bare. So they will fall down and worship God, exclaiming, "God is really among you! (1 Corinthians 14:18-25).

Paul is advocating for discernment from the Corinthians so they don't choke the gift of the Spirit but continue to speak in tongues for personal edification and prayer. He also makes a point of how the public tongue from the church pulpit is being interpreted so they don't just babble (verses 19-21).

Many things could be different in the church today if we took time to teach people about spiritual gifts and to train them so they would know how to use them. If Paul did it, we can do it. Do people make mistakes? Oh, yes. But how can people learn if they don't try? God gave us a gift of discernment to use if people make mistakes!

In Most Perfect Order
The conclusion of chapter 14 is found in verse 26: All spiritual gifts are to be used, but it is important that it is done in order to edify the church.

What then shall we say, brothers and sisters? When you come together, each of you has a hymn, or a word of instruction, a revelation, a tongue or an interpretation. Everything must be done so that the church may be built up (1 Corinthians 14:26).

We even get guidelines on how it should be done:

If anyone speaks in a tongue, two—or at the most three—should speak, one at a time, and someone must interpret. If there is no interpreter, the speaker should keep quiet in the church and speak to himself and to God. Two or three prophets should speak, and the others should weigh carefully what is said. And if a revelation comes to someone who is sitting down, the first speaker should stop. For you can all prophesy in turn so that everyone may be instructed and encouraged. The spirits of prophets are subject to the control of prophets. For God is not a God of disorder but of peace—as in all the congregations of the Lord's people (1 Corinthians 14:27-33).

The other day, someone stood up in church and spoke in tongues which does not happen very often in our congregation. I did not know the man who delivered the message but I looked around to see if someone had the interpretation. One of our pastors stood up and interpreted the message and, after the service, another co-worker came to me and told me that he also had an interpretation. Paul says if someone has a prophetic message in tongues which can be interpreted, it should be limited to two or three people. If there is nobody who can interpret, then it's better to just speak in tongues personally rather than speaking out in a prophetic tongue.

Prophetic messages are always to be discerned. The spirit of a prophet is subject to the prophet, meaning you can easily control when to deliver your message, and it is not "unspiritual" to direct it as this is happening. You can wait until it is your turn. It is important that everybody conforms to the prophetic anointing without any confusion.

A Command From The Lord
I have chosen to go through 1 Corinthians 14 systematically because this chapter is very important for us to understand. Paul says that this is not something that he just came up with by himself, but that it is a command from the Lord!

> *If anyone thinks they are a prophet or otherwise gifted by the Spirit, let them acknowledge that what I am writing to you is the Lord's command. But if anyone ignores this, they will themselves be ignored. Therefore, my brothers and sisters, be eager to prophesy, and do not forbid speaking in tongues. But everything should be done in a fitting and orderly way (1 Corinthians 14:37-40).*

It's scary how this teaching has been used to shut down speaking in tongues in some churches. Instead of growing the gifts, they control the gifts by putting the emphasis on the last verse, "Let all things be done decently and in order." There is a maturity that needs to take place. We should not control the working of the Spirit out of fear of losing control. Better to try something rather than not try it at all. Why should He give us the gifts of the Spirit if they were not meant to be used? God is calling us to take a step of faith. The gifts are not given to you to keep them. They are given to you to use them.

Chapter 12

THE TELEPHONE POLE

But when he, the Spirit of Truth, comes, He will guide you into all the truth. He will not speak on his own; He will speak only what He hears, and He will tell you what is yet to come. He will glorify Me because it is from Me that he will receive what He will make known to you (John 16:13-14).

When we pray for people to receive the baptism of the Holy Spirit, we don't give up. We keep praying until something happens so that no one should walk away disappointed, thinking they were among the few who never get to experience the power of God's breakthrough in their lives.

Too many disappointments will make you negative towards the Holy Spirit and you will end up as a member of what I used to call the "Telephone Pole Club". The definition of a telephone pole is a Christian, standing still and tall, while everyone else is laying on the floor under the power of God. Christians in the "Telephone Pole Club" are erect and religious with everything under control, pressure-creosoted and, apparently, completely untouchable to God's Holy Spirit.

Begin, Begin, Begin

I was once invited to speak in a meeting especially for such "telephone pole Christians". It was a very interesting gathering of people from all kinds of different places and churches, coming together because they had heard that on this special evening God would share His good gifts kindly with everybody, without reproach.

People thought they were coming to a regular revival meeting, but we changed the setting from church to classroom-style, turning all chairs and tables around so that people would know they were there to be taught. As I began teaching, I made sure that everyone had a Bible. I wanted them to understand that, without the Word, nothing would happen. The breakthrough is always found in the Word.

After the teaching, we called the utility pole people forward to receive prayer. More than 30 people stood up. I knew that some of them had been searching for the power without the evidence of speaking in tongues for over 20 years.

As they were standing there, the Holy Spirit came. Instantly, half of the "telephone poles" was filled with the power of God, praising Him in new tongues. This was amazing! It was spreading like wildfire. One after another, they received their spiritual language as they heard the others speaking in tongues. You could almost feel how faith was growing in the room.

In the end, only one person was left. I could see how he was looking around, having this nervous look on his face as he was standing there all by himself. I did not have to be a prophet to read his mind. I asked him, and he was already planning to go home empty-handed.

"Tonight is your night, and you are going to receive something, just like everybody else. Start speaking in tongues." I continued.

The man started praying in his native tongue.

"Fill me up God. Fill me up. Won't you just fill me up, please!" as if God would hear him because of the many words he said.

I told him to stop speaking regular words. No more "Thank you Jesus" and "Hallelujah."

"How many mouths do you have?" I asked the man.

The poor guy was staring at me and I really hoped that he would understand my point.

"You only have one mouth. How can you beg God in your own language while you are supposed to use that same mouth to speak in tongues at the same time?"

Suddenly, he understood. He stopped speaking in his native tongue and chose to use his mouth to speak in tongues he did not understand. He spoke only a few words but it was still enough to convince him the new language he was speaking came from God, and not from himself.

When I met him two weeks later he told me he still had the same words. I asked if he would like to receive more and, as we prayed, he received a full language.

The next time, he came together with his wife. Now they could pray in tongues together and they explained how their lives and their marriage had been turned upside down. After the baptism of the Holy Spirit, they never had a boring moment.

"It's like going 100 miles an hour!" they explained.

Luther Is Dead

As revival was breaking out, we had a lot of young people coming to our house. One of them was a young girl from the Evangelical Lutheran church. She loved Jesus, but she was spiritually dry because of all the anti-Holy Spirit teaching she had received. She had so many theological opinions and explanations that you would almost start sneezing from the dust flying out of her mouth!

When we met her, she was planning to travel to Asia on a summer mission project and then begin her studies at the University of Copenhagen. But what she didn't know was that God was about to change her destiny.

One evening, we began talking about the baptism of the Holy Spirit and tongues. It was obvious that she had her own opinions, but I could also tell that she was hungry for God. Together, we read the Word and, this time, she gave up discussing and ended up letting us pray for her.

The first hour we prayed, nothing happened. We tried to make her cooperate with us in many different ways, but those old religious ways of thinking - the religious strongholds in her mind - were like brick walls. It was almost impossible to break through them.

After two hours, my wife was starting to get tired. But the very thought of leaving this wonderful young lady even more bound and condemned than before gave us boldness and patience to continue to speak faith and believe in God's Word and promises.

After three hours, I was getting tired. We had decreed and declared, rebuked, broken and bound and, so far, nothing tangible had happened. I was confused. I was used to casting out demons but it seemed like this particular one would not go.

As I stood there, the Holy Spirit showed me this was not a demon. What I was up against was many years of religious teaching and tradition. When I realized this, I found myself responding in a very non-religious and untraditional way!

"Die Luther," I exclaimed.

I couldn't believe what came out of my mouth but this time it worked. The girl immediately started praising God in new tongues, was filled with the Holy Spirit and ended up changing all of her perfect plans for the future.

Instead of going to Asia, she went to Africa and got a job as a volunteer at an orphanage. She even married one of my good friends and, until this day, they have a powerful ministry taking care of children and orphans in Uganda.

"Speak African"

One day, I was out roller-skating when I met a young man. He and I were at the hockey grounds and, on the ramps, this young man argued against the baptism of the Holy Spirit and the gift of tongues. There was just one problem: He was hungry and wanted more of Jesus.

We became friends and he ended up going home to our house to hear more about spiritual things. I realized that he was just as Lutheran as the young girl we had prayed for so, instead of discussing the baptism of the Holy Spirit, we tried to serve the message in a seeker-friendly way wrapped in the right Lutheran terms so he could discover the gift. This was before I learned that it was much easier just to be straightforward with the Truth.

The first hour passed. We were begging God to do something unusual and, when nothing happened in the next hour, my wife went to bed. Since then, she has learned to be more persistent. How can you go to sleep when you are praying for revival and want to partake in what God wants to do in a nation?

I continued praying and trusting God, quoting the Scripture about how He rewards those who seek Him diligently. It seemed like my bed screamed louder than the Word of God. I was so tired, and my friend still didn't dare to open his mouth. It was way past midnight and I was pretty frustrated. Out of pure desperation, I suggested to him to speak African.

"I don't know how to speak African," he said.

"Just open your mouth and say something that sounds African." I said.

I cannot theologically explain what happened. But when he switched off his brain and gave in, he immediately started speaking in new tongues. He was set on fire for Jesus and the fire spread around him. Today, he and his friends are evangelizing in the streets. Many people have met Jesus through his life and ministry.

Bible Camping

Due to all the testimonies, I received an invitation to preach in a Lutheran convention about the baptism of the Holy Spirit which was very unusual. As I was teaching, I used a lot of the Scriptures from this book. Then I started calling people forward to be baptized in the Holy Spirit.

First, I made an altar call for people who were smoking.

"If you have come here today to receive the Holy Spirit, you must be willing to lay down your cigarettes," I said.

Some people would rather have their cigarettes than the baptism of the Holy Spirit. Some returned to their seats. I prayed for those who were still at the front. As they repented from cigarettes, having one foot in the world and one foot in the church, they were filled with the Holy Spirit and started speaking in tongues.

Afterwards, we went to another room where we could get more personal with people. There were about 15-20 people sitting in a circle and, one by one, they received the gift of tongues including one of the veterans. He had been at the convention every year without receiving the gift of the Holy Spirit. He believed that speaking in tongues would never work for him.

Finally, there was only one person left--a young woman with a sad face who now had become even more sad as she was the last person left in the circle who hadn't started speaking in tongues.

Instead of speaking in tongues, I started speaking to her in other languages. I told her how to say "I love you, Jesus" in Danish, Swedish, English, French, Spanish, German, Russian, Hebrew, Swahili etc., and she repeated every sentence after me.

At one point, I started to speak to her in tongues and, again, she repeated after me. When she realized she had been speaking in tongues (my personal tongues) she was shocked. I could almost see smoke from her brain coming out of her ears but, instead of giving up, she kept going.

She really wanted the gift and now, by repeating after me, the fear was gone. I kept praying and told her to speak loud and clear until the breakthrough came.

I told her to sit in a corner and speak secrets with God which she did for a long time as she was crying. After that, she testified about how God had healed the pain in her heart. Nine years ago, she lost a child and, after that traumatic experience, she had been in a mental ward for therapy. For all of those nine years, she was not able to be among other people, particularly parents with their kids.

The Holy Spirit made the whole difference: The next day, she was able to be among other people again, and she had no problem being with kids! The depression was gone. She was no longer sad but truly happy, inside and out, completely free! What doctors and psychiatrists hadn't been able to do through medical treatment, the Holy Spirit fixed in just one afternoon and she was immediately dismissed from mental therapy!

In the Roundabout
In the same convention we met a couple from a non-denominational church. She was baptized in the Holy Spirit, but he didn't speak in tongues though he had tried many times. It was not the theology that was blocking him, but all of the bad experiences and disappointments every time he had been prayed for and nothing had happened.

I could feel his hunger for more. One day, when I was going out to minister in a church close by, he went with me in the car. I had the opportunity to teach him as we traveled on our way. Our trip of 30 kilometers was just enough for me to show him the Scriptures about the baptism of the Holy Spirit and tongues.

As we were on our way home from the meeting, I challenged his faith.

"If you have asked, you have also received. God will not give you a stone when you're asking for bread," I said.

I was busy keeping my eyes on the road and slowed down as we were about to enter a roundabout. There were four lamp posts in the roundabout, and I pointed at one of them:

"When we reach that lamp post over there, you are going to speak in tongues! I said.

The man looked at me. Many thoughts went through his head. When we passed the first lamp post he didn't say a word. At the second lamp post, he started speaking in tongues. He was hesitant at first but gradually, he became more and more convincing. When we got home, he was so drunk in the Spirit that he couldn't stand on his legs. He rolled out of the car to the courtyard where he was praising God in tongues on the ground, unaware of what was going on around him. The power of God had hit him so hard, he was completely drunk in the Spirit!

We managed to get him up from the ground, put him in the prayer room and agreed that he could stay there and sleep until he was "back on earth" again. I don't know how long he stayed in there but, when he finally made it home to his wife, she was very surprised to see him in that condition. She had never seen him that way before, but she was happy to see that he had finally gotten the breakthrough that he had dreamed of for so many years.

The next morning, he was completely changed. So was his marriage because now he and his wife were able to have a deeper spiritual fellowship together. Many things have happened since then and he is a real man of God today!

Fear of Fake Tongues

I had another experience with a young girl, who had a burning desire to experience the baptism of the Holy Spirit. Because of her Lutheran background she wouldn't call it baptism and, because of her fear of it being fake, she didn't dare to try speak in tongues.

Just like a lot of other people, she did not believe that she was worthy to receive the gift. She had learned that tongues was a gift of the Spirit that was given exclusively to intercessors and, when she didn't exactly feel called to be an intercessor, it made her sad and scared.

She came to one of our meetings. I asked if she spoke in tongues. She said she wanted to, so I opened the Bible and started to teach. I showed her most of the Scriptures in the Bible saying that tongues is for everyone. Finally, she stopped arguing.

When we came to Mark 16:16 which said "these signs shall follow those who believe," I challenged her.

"How can you say you believe when you don't speak in tongues?" I asked.

Suddenly, revelation from the Holy Spirit made her realize there was no way to escape. The young girl chose to submit herself to the Word of God as she was crying in anger because her religion and false doctrines were shown to be in error.

We went next door where I gave her a few more Scriptures. Then, I asked the Holy Spirit to come. I counted to three and, immediately, she started speaking in tongues with tears streaming down her face and the religious smoke puffed out of her ears.

All at one time, she received a full language and experienced great release. The girl went home that night. We met the following day with her. She told us she had been attacked by fear of it all just having been something she had made up out of her own imagination. She didn't dare to believe that it really was God who had given her this wonderful language! The battle in her mind continued for months but, instead of stopping the tongues, she kept on submitting herself to the Word of God. Today she doesn't have a bit of doubt in her mind that God gives the Holy Spirit to everybody, including the gift of speaking in tongues.

Chapter 13

THIRST COMES FIRST

On the last and greatest day of the festival, Jesus stood and said in a loud voice, "Let anyone who is thirsty come to me and drink. Whoever believes in me, as Scripture has said, rivers of living water will flow from within them." By this he meant the Spirit, whom those who believed in him were later to receive. Up to that time the Spirit had not been given, since Jesus had not yet been glorified (John 7:37-39).

If you are thirsty you drink. If you are not thirsty you don't drink. Thirst comes first. Thirst is what qualifies you to receive. In order to experience the baptism of the Holy Spirit you must have spiritual thirst after the living water that God wants to give to you.

Maybe you know the quote, "you can lead a horse to water but you can't make it drink." This is not a proverb in the Bible but a well known saying, which means you can give someone the opportunity to do something, but you cannot force them to do it if they do not want to.

When my dog is thirsty, nothing can hold him back from drinking. If the water bowl is empty he runs desperately around and tries to give us signals he is thirsty. Sometimes he'll march around the kitchen with the empty water bowl in his mouth. On other occasions, I have seen him drink from the water in the toilet. Or he would run all the way down to the lake to get water. His great desire for water would always make a way for him to quench his thirst, and be satisfied.

The Holy Spirit wants to fill you to a point where you overflow. I can tell you about how wonderful water is, but I can't force you to drink. It is my prayer that this book has made you so thirsty that you can't keep yourself from drinking the living water that He has provided for us as believers. A thirsty person puts everything aside to get a drink. Nothing is more important when you feel as dry as the desert!

God sees the spiritual thirst and desire in your heart. Natural water is important for your natural life, but the water of the Holy Spirit is important for your spiritual life. There is an inner thirst that cannot be quenched without the Holy Spirit. When we drink from the water of the Holy Spirit, you will never thirst again.

But whoever drinks the water I give them will never thirst. Indeed, the water I give them will become in them a spring of water welling up to eternal life (John 4:14).

Come to Jesus

It is very simple to come to Jesus. Go to your room and shut the door, or go for a walk in beautiful nature and find a place where you can be alone. Turn off your cell phone and close your eyes so that it's easier for you to concentrate. When you're in this position, ask Jesus to baptize you with the Holy Spirit, giving you the gift of tongues as a sign.

You must come to Jesus in order to receive the Holy Spirit. He is the one who baptizes with Spirit and fire. Seek Him. Have a stubborn attitude. Don't give up until you've received what you've asked for. Maybe you need to talk to some Spirit-filled people about what you've read in this book. If you don't know how to come to Jesus, then go to the house of God - some place where they speak in tongues - and ask them to lay hands on you so that you can receive the baptism of the Holy Spirit.

Jesus says that the one who comes to Him will by no means be cast out.

All those the Father gives me will come to me, and whoever comes to me I will never drive away (John 6:37).

Drink From the Well

Jesus gives rivers of living water to all who are thirsty and come to Him. The Holy Spirit is not for super

Christians, but for thirsty souls who have chosen to submit their lives to the guidance of the Word of God.

When we want to receive the baptism of the Holy Spirit we must follow the instruction. Jesus doesn't just say "Come." He also says "Drink." If you are thirsty, it's not enough just to know there is water in the faucet. You must also know the way to the faucet and how to turn the handle for water to come forth. When you stand in front of the faucet, you must take a step to open your mouth and drink, or your thirst won't be quenched! How do you do that? Simply by opening your mouth and starting to speak. God has promised to fill our mouth when we open it:

I am the LORD your God, who brought you up out of Egypt. Open wide your mouth and I will fill it (Psalm 81:10).

He will yet fill your mouth with laughter and your lips with shouts of joy (Job 8:21).

When you begin to speak in tongues, don't focus on the gift. Focus on the Giver. Ask the Spirit to reveal Jesus to you. That is His job, to make Jesus known and to make Jesus great! Imagine yourself standing in front of Jesus thanking Him for all He has done.

When your own words come to an end, let your heart flow over with the most wonderful words. Tell Him how much you love Him, from the deep of your spirit to the deep of His Spirit. Let the waves of the Holy Spirit sweep over you!

Deep calls to deep in the roar of your waterfalls; all your waves and breakers have swept over me (Psalm 42:7).

If you have a hard time expressing the language of the Spirit, try to sing it out. Some people find it easier to sing it out than to speak. If you feel that way, then sing first and speak afterwards. The most important thing is to get started.

Believe His Word

The moment you start speaking in tongues, you must have faith in His Word. Don't allow yourself to be distracted. The first thought that comes to you might be to question whether this is really from God or not, and this is where faith must be plugged in.

"Those who believe..." Jesus says. It is not enough to hope for it to happen. You must choose to have faith in His Word and believe in His promises to receive the language of the Spirit. Faith is the bucket that draws the water from the well.

And without faith it is impossible to please God, because anyone who comes to Him must believe that He exists and that He rewards those who earnestly seek Him (Hebrews 11:6).

If you are a believer, you are also a receiver. Faith without actions is dead. Faith will not settle for less. Faith comes from what is heard by the power of the Word of God. If the Word of God says that He wants to baptize you with the Holy Spirit, have faith in His Word. Nothing is impossible. Have faith in God.

Just as you received Jesus by faith, you must receive the Holy Spirit by faith:

For it is with your heart that you believe and are justified, and it is with your mouth that you profess your faith and are saved (Romans 10:10).

Whatever is in your heart must come out of your mouth. If the Spirit of God lives in your heart and you are a temple for His Spirit by believing in His Name, the words coming out of your mouth must, therefore, also be inspired by the Spirit of God.

Living Water
Before you continue reading, ask Jesus to baptize you in the Holy Spirit by reading this prayer out loud.

"Dear Jesus!
I ask you to baptize me with Holy Spirit and fire. I ask you to give me the gift of tongues as a sign. I thank you, Jesus, for not giving me a stone when I'm asking for bread, and that you gladly give the Holy Spirit to those who ask. Quench my thirst and fill me with your living water. Amen."

Imagine how Jesus opens for the water. Can you feel it bubbling? Let it flow. Let it cleanse you and tear down the blockages in your system. God will let His fresh, living water flow from your life and from my life. Living water can't stand still. It carries a force in itself -

the power of the Spirit which creates results. Consider how much energy there is in a waterfall or a tsunami! If you are thirsty, listen to the guidance of the Holy Spirit when He says: "Come and drink."

As Christians we don't need to drink alcohol to feel happiness. We have another "Spirit," the Holy Spirit of God from which we can always drink without getting hang overs! When we come to Him, He will give us living water, free of charge. He wants to fill us, not just once, but continuously with new provision again and again as the water, His living water, overflows to the people that are around us.

Nothing compares to that living water. Come to Him. Drink and have faith in His Word, and you will experience the Spirit of God burst forth in your life with great power.

The Spirit and the bride say, "Come!" And let the one who hears say, "Come!" Let the one who is thirsty come; and let the one who wishes take the free gift of the water of life (Revelation 22:17).

May God bless you with the baptism and language of the Holy Spirit.

EPILOGUE

Turn at my rebuke; Surely I will pour out my spirit on you; I will make my words known to you (Proverbs 1:23 NKJV).

God has promised to pour out the Holy Spirit on you: He will make His words known to you as you seek knowledge, He gives knowledge, He is the source of knowledge and wisdom!

If you would like to know more about the Holy Spirit and the language of the Spirit, go to our Facebook page, Holy Spirit Wildfire, and look for the prayer link.

I have recorded my personal prayer time with words taught by the Spirit. If you want to know what it sounds like, you can click on the link and pray together with me.

Sincerely,

Christian Hedegaard

Pastor Christian Hedegaard
Powerhouse Church
Orlando, FL

ABOUT THE AUTHOR

Christian Hedegaard was born in 1966 in Denmark, went to Bible College in Copenhagen, and started as a full-time minister of the gospel in 1996. He has been married to Karen Hedegaard since 1988, and is the father of four children.

Christian Hedegaard has traveled to more than 60 nations, preaching the gospel and planting churches. In 2000, he started an evangelistic ministry that had a significant impact in his home country.

Additionally, he is a recording artist, and the author of six books among which his first book, *Conquering Demons,* was translated into five languages and published in the USA in 2014.

In December 2011, Christian Hedegaard and his family moved to Orlando, Florida, to work among the homeless. Today he is the founder and pastor of Powerhouse Church on Orange Blossom Trail, a poverty stricken area in downtown Orlando. The church is open six days a week and serves food, provides clothes, and gives housing and legal help people in need.

If this book has helped you to receive the baptism of the Holy Spirit with the evidence of speaking in tongues, please send your testimony to the following address:

Powerhouse Church
1025 S Orange Blossom Trail
Orlando, FL 32805
www.powerhouseflorida.com
info@powerhouseflorida.com

Made in the USA
Columbia, SC
13 October 2023

24040820R00090